Mother
Wit

Mother Wit

A Feminist Guide
to Psychic Development
by
Diane Mariechild

THE CROSSING PRESS / Trumansburg, New York 14886

I want to thank Karen Lindsey whose support, energy and fine editing skills were truly blessings in the preparation of this book. Many thanks to Jake Flaherty, Marc Maloof, Mike Flaherty and Kevin Welsh for their help in writing the children's section. Thanks also to Seija Ling and Marian Clark for believing in my psychic abilities and Sue Silvermarie for believing in my strength as a writer. And a special thanks to Anne Lewis for the song in her heart. AXOKE.

This work comes from many sources including women who are unknown to me but whose images and chants have been passed through workshops and ritual gatherings.

Cover design by Mary A. Scott
Cover photographs by Cheryl Sena
Book illustrations by Kim Thomsen
Photograph of Diane Mariechild by Amtul Hannan

Printed in the U.S.A.

ISBN: 0-89594-051-5 paper
ISBN: 0-89594-050-7 cloth
L.C. No. 81-4159

This is dedicated to the one I love.

Contents

Introduction

BACKGROUND

I have been actively involved in developing my psychic skills since first becoming part of a Womancraft class in February of 1974. Participating in that workshop was the beginning of an incredible experience. I discovered a way of traveling deep within myself, uncovering parts of myself I hadn't known existed. I learned to create a special mind-space where I could listen to my inner voices, use my fantasies to solve problems, heal whatever was wrong with my physical body and reach a clearer understanding of my dreams. What these exercises have done for me, I believe, they can do for others.

There were eight women in the Womancraft workshop I attended. We assembled early in the evening, carrying sleeping bags to lie on while we moved into the trance state. I didn't know what would occur, having been told only that this class would help me develop psychically.

Most of what happened that evening is a hazy memory. The lights were dimmed, we lay quietly and the guide's soothing voice drifted over us, instructing us to relax each part of our bodies. As the exercises continued, I was able to move quickly and easily into the trance state. What we learned might at first seem silly if you've never experienced it. We learned how to project our consciousness into a plant and communicate with it; we met two spirit guides or counselors, upon whom we could call whenever we needed advice and support; we became sensitive to healing energy and learned to send it throughout our bodies and into the bodies of our friends. The most amazing exercise, for me, was psychic diagnosis. My partner guided me into the trance state and then gave me the name of a woman who was unknown to me. I concentrated on her and was able to diagnose her physical and emotional state accurately. Of course, I had always believed other people could do this, the psychics, but I never thought *I* could.

Womancraft had its beginnings in Boston in the spring of 1973. Several women had taken the Silva Mind Control Course and found it helpful but male-oriented in goals and language. They wanted to use their new skills in a feminist way. They saw that a course encouraging psychic awareness would be a helpful way of validating and using the traditionally female qualities (emotionalism, sensitivity, receptivity and passivity). They understood that female energies are not valued in our patriarchal society. Instead, male values of law and order and rational thought are valued, and attempts are made to harness the powers of nature. Men assume the dominant role in this society: a father-god is worshipped, the father is the head of the family, the blood line is traced through the males and property is personal rather than communal.

Today the ancient matriarchal principle is reasserting its power. This is *eros,* the female spiritual or psychological principle of love, unity and peace. The laws of the matriarchate are the laws of nature and instinct: the inner life of feelings and emotions is highly valued. Life is seen as cyclical, a continually rearranging balance. The earth is sacred, giving birth and sustenance to all that is. Nature is the teacher, revealing the mysteries of life. Nature is not a power to be harnessed or overcome.

We need to reclaim our female side, but not in the old unconscious way. We must learn new ways of integrating and balancing both female and male energies. These are not opposing poles but complementary manifestations of the same life force. We need to learn to express both energies in appropriate ways.

Womancraft helped me to discover how I could do this. Those women and their beautiful vision created a workshop that enhanced women's strengths and women's intuitions.

Excited by the many possibilities the workshop opened to me, I continued to explore psychic spaces with a friend. Meeting several hours each week and using the Masters and Housten book *Mind Games** as a guide, Jane and I explored other realms of awareness. Sometimes other people joined us, but for the most part it remained just the two of us. We were soon creating our own exercises to help focus our energy. In the trance state we explored our dreams, our fantasies and our past lives. We examined our beliefs. We concentrated on sending out positive thoughts, thus making our lives take a more affirmative direction. We began paying closer attention to our bodies' messages, recognizing the how and why of physical ill-

---

*Robert Masters and Jean Housten, *Mind Games* (New York: Viking Press, 1972).

ness. We practiced sending healing energy to each other and to friends who requested it.

As my consciousness about healing and disease expanded, I shared this knowledge with my children. In our discussions we learned how we create illness (getting a sore throat when words are caught in our throats, getting a stomach-ache when we don't want to go to school or work), and began learning more appropriate ways of expressing our feelings and needs. When someone got sick we sent them healing, using laying on of hands and visual images. Bedtime became a time of magical journeys to faraway places. The children came to rely more on themselves, as they were able to call upon the friend inside them. We talked about our lives, the directions we wanted to take and how we could use our mind power to make those changes happen. Rather than worrying about failures, we focused on positive outcomes. Family meetings were opened with energy circles. We created several rituals for releasing fears and directing positive energy.

At the same time my work as a feminist counselor was enriched. I used trance states with my clients in the same ways I used them for myself: working on dreams, self-healing, problem-solving, releasing fears, focusing and directing energy. I also shared my growing ability to interpret the body's messages and to use breath energy and visual images to heal.

My dream recall increased. I also became more alert while in the dream state so that I could direct the images consciously. Moving easily between waking and dreaming states, I became more attuned to my intuitive mind.

As I grew more sensitive to the different levels of energy, I felt a resurgence of a spiritual awareness, this time in a subtler, more woman-oriented way. At times I visualize this cosmic energy as the Great Mother, and use my meditations as a way of connecting with this life force. The daily practice of Hatha Yoga and meditation has enabled me to become clear. Often I receive information through my spirit guides—an Egyptian woman and an Oriental man.

Ritual has assumed an important part in my life: lighting of candles and incense during meditation; visualizing a rainbow of light surrounding and protecting me; creating a magic circle where I can release tension and fear and become filled with love, affirming the strength of my own being.

I began studying mythology and the ancient matriarchal religions and, with a group of friends, created rituals of release, affirmation and creation. Meeting each month when the moon is full, a time of great psychic energy, we expanded our celebrations to include the Greater and Lesser Sabats of the Wiccan calendar.

Since my initial contact with the Womancraft workshop, I have continued to explore and develop my psychic and healing abilities. Meditation, *yoga,* talks with my Oversoul and my spirit guides, solitary and group rituals have all become an important part of my life. I continue working with clients as a psychotherapist, as well as teaching several psychic skills classes weekly at the beginning and intermediate levels. I also see people individually for *chakra* readings, past life regressions, healing and psychic development. As I look back over the last few years, I see how I was guided to the Womancraft workshop so that in this life I might continue to develop psychically and share that development with others. What I have learned most is to appreciate myself, to understand my own ways of growing and sharing and to accept both my strengths and my weaknesses. I am able to move more often from a clear space within myself, from my center.

PSYCHIC AWARENESS

Psyche, the Greek word for soul, refers to things beyond the known physical world. Psychic information does not come from the five senses. There is nothing crazy or weird about psychic ability, nor is it some rare gift. We are all psychic.

The exercises in this book are designed to help you explore and develop psychic awareness that comes to you through your intuitions, hunches, feelings and body sensations. It includes the phenomena of hearing voices, seeing images and symbols and perceiving auras. By following the exercises outlined here, you will become able to relax and center yourself in the trance state where you are in touch with your intuitive powers. You will learn to protect yourself by strengthening your aura, the electromagnetic field which surrounds you. You will practice healing, gather information about other lives, learn to direct your energy at will and participate in womanrituals. These activities, however, are not ends in themselves. We increase our psychic awareness as a way of aiding our own evolution, and thereby the evolution of the whole human race.

We are all familiar with rational knowing: the ability to analyze, focus and separate. Western, patriarchal society has overemphasized reason, telling us this is the only way to learn. We women have swallowed this male way of seeing the world. We have idolized logical thought, worshipped reason and in the process severed the connection with our souls, the deepest layers of our psyches. It is this connection we must struggle to remake.

We must relearn and re-remember sources of information that patriarchal society has, for thousands of years, denied. We must begin to appreciate anew our female qualities, that diffused awareness that allows us to read between the lines and sense the connections between all living things. We must look with new respect at the importance of the inner worlds, feelings and intuitions. In so doing we come to realize the importance of passivity, the brooding* and nurturing attitude from which springs the eternal source of creativity. It is only when we reconnect with this female principle and affirm it within ourselves and within society that we come into our own power, womanpower.

A WORD ABOUT ETHICS

Psychic abilities, once developed, are very powerful. When we begin to take our own energy seriously, we become accountable to universal laws. The first law is: the energy that you send out always comes back to you. If you act in a violent way, you become violent; if you act in a peaceful way, you become peaceful. Giving and receiving are two sides of the same coin. *Karma,* the law of cause and effect, is linked to the concept of reincarnation. This balance of energy, this give and take, is evened out over many lifetimes. You can't always see the results of your actions in your present lifetime.

The second law of energy is: the greater your awareness, the greater your responsibilities. You can either act out of a space of love and abundance or you can act out of a space of fear and limitation. You cannot act from both spaces simultaneously. Psychic abilities must always be used in a loving and non-violent way. It is never acceptable to use psychic abilities to manipulate or assume power over others.

Living in a world where violence and injustice are so much a part of everyday life, it is hard not to be tempted to use psychic abilities to retaliate. Such feelings are understandable. However, we have all perpetuated the use of violence either by actively harming others or by ignoring our own needs, thereby allowing ourselves to be harmed. We must learn to use power in loving, peaceful ways. Violence—that is, *power over*—must be stopped. Our intentions create the results. The following situations are examples of what I consider to be ethical and unethical ways of dealing psychically with difficult situations.

1. Your friend is sick. You feel that she would benefit by having a different diet. So you project those thoughts into her mind. This is an invasion of her psychic space. Everyone has the right to their own illnesses. To decide what someone needs, however good your intentions, is assuming power over them. It is better to send your friend positive energy which she can accept if she wishes and use as she wishes.

---

*I use "brood" in its positive sense of dwelling and focusing on something in an intense way that enables it to grow and expand. To brood: to nourish, to nurture, to hatch.

2. You are feeling very lonely and have been without a lover for some time. You know someone with whom you wish to become involved. Should you relax, deepen and visualize yourself involved with this person in a conscious attempt to bring this about? No, because this would also be manipulative. To place another person in a specific situation without their knowledge is assuming power over them and is a form of mental violence. It would be better to visualize yourself involved with a wonderful, compatible person whom you don't know. What you really want is a close, intimate relationship with someone. You may think that only a certain person would make you happy, but this isn't true. It is important for you to examine closely what you really want and why.

3. You are involved in a relationship and wish to improve communication. Do not project commands into the other person's mind. To improve communication work on yourself, since ultimately *you* are the only person you can change. You can use "creative visualization" to imagine yourself becoming calmer and more patient or communicating your needs more directly.

4. You have been raped. Should you send negative energy to the rapist, hoping that he will break his leg, or worse? No, to do that would only perpetuate the violence as well as bind you to him because of the intense emotion. If you use mental violence against someone else, you are leaving

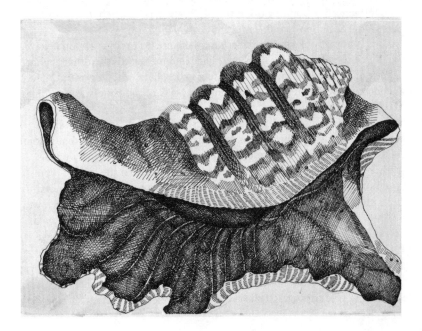

yourself open to being the recipient of someone else's mental violence. Surrounding yourself with white light and using affirmations to acknowledge your health, strength and wisdom are two ways of protecting yourself psychically. (This, of course, does not eliminate the need for protection on the physical level: having strong locks on your doors and learning self-defense.) If you have been the victim of a violent attack, it is important to confront your fear and anger and learn to release them.

5. You are unemployed and about to be interviewed for a job that seems right for you. Should you direct the interviewer mentally to hire you? No, this would be manipulation. If you know the interviewer's name, you can visit her the night before the interview in your "astral" (see Chapter Four) and tell her why you think she should hire you. The next day the interviewer may very well feel that you have met before. Right before the interview you can deepen and center yourself and affirm that you will intuitively respond to the questions in the most effective way.

HOW TO USE THIS BOOK

This book contains a series of practical exercises to facilitate the development of your natural psychic and healing abilities. All of the exercises have evolved out of my own experience, individually and with groups, and have been influenced by, among other things, Womancraft, Witchcraft, *Mind Games,* the Seth books and *Hatha* and *Kundalini Yoga.*

This is not a book of proofs because there are no proofs. If you believe that something is true if it can be weighed and measured, then that is your belief. Each of us lives by a set of values and beliefs, whether or not they are consciously articulated. This book is a book of my beliefs, those things that have proven true for me.

These beliefs are not absolute: they grow and change as I grow and change. Truth is not absolute or permanent. (You may believe that if something lasts a long time it is true, but that is your belief: longevity equals truth.) Each of us creates a circle around ourselves, and the circle is composed of our attitudes, feelings and beliefs. This is necessary for survival and a good idea as long as we are comfortable within that circle. When we no longer feel comfortable we can change that circle: erase it and draw a new one. Our circles are magic—they allow us to grow freely and change. If the circles become absolute and rigid, we become trapped by our beliefs and no longer are free.

So I ask you to join my circle for a while, to try out my beliefs and see if they ring true for you. If they do, you are welcome to them: if not, cast them aside and create your own. It is not necessary for you to believe as I do in order for these exercises to work for you. Move at your own pace, try our the exercises that feel comfortable and when you are ready try others.

If you are working alone, read the exercise through to familiarize yourself with it. Then relax, center, deepen, protect yourself (see Chapter One) and practice. If you have a tape recorder available, you may want to make tapes of certain exercises. To make a tape read the exercise slowly so that you will have enough space to experience each part of the exercise.

It is a good idea to work with other women as you develop your psychic abilities so that you can support each other. But your greatest support must come from yourself. You must believe these techniques will work in order for them to work. This may be very hard for you. We have been raised to believe that we don't deserve what we want and we can't trust what we want. We have been raised to believe that psychic energy cannot possibly change anything.

These techniques allow yourself to trust that still, small voice that says, "This might work and I'll try it." This is a new way of perceiving. New ideas often take a while to feel comfortable. Try saying to yourself, "There is a part of me that believes this is silly. I really don't have the power to change my life, but while I practice this exercise, I'm going to lay that part aside and listen to the part of me that says there might be something to this and I'll give that part a chance to grow." Gradually as you change your beliefs you will find that your outer life is changing also.

If a technique isn't working for you, ask yourself if it is really something that you want to do. Perhaps it is not the appropriate time for you to be making that kind of change. If you find you really do want to make the change, then maybe you find succeeding more threatening than failing. Many of us have been conditioned to think of ourselves as victims. To realize that we have the power to change can be frightening.

It takes time and effort to learn how to deepen into the trance state. After a few times you will become familiar with the sensations. Sometimes your eyelids flutter; your body may feel either very heavy or very light; you might feel cool; you may feel as though you are dreaming. There is no one way you will feel.

Practice when you are relaxed. Once you get accustomed to moving into the trance state, it will be easier to do it at times when you are not so relaxed. Then you'll be able to use it to help relax. If you feel that you never really relax, don't worry. Practice deepening yourself a little each day and soon it will come.

At first try practicing for short periods of time, five or ten minutes. To make it a habit, take very small steps, doing only as much as you know you *will* do. This way your success is assured. As you work toward disciplining yourself to daily practice, remember to remain flexible. Let the structure evolve from within you, not by forcing from the outside. Some days it won't work at all. That's okay—the attempt is important. Sometimes you won't feel like doing it for a while. That's okay too: allow yourself the freedom to change the schedule. Who said you have to do it every day to make it work?

If you fall asleep when you are practicing, that's usually because you needed the sleep. If this continues and it interrupts your practice, tell yourself that you will remain awake and alert during the exercise. Or practice the exercise sitting up.

If you see an image that is frightening, or one that you don't like, simply blink your eyes and it will disappear. Or say to the image, "Go in peace." If the experience is very unpleasant, open your eyes and sit up. You will return instantly.

If you feel an excess of energy after doing any exercise and you don't know how to channel it, try shaking your hands vigorously and then placing them, palms down, on the floor to ground them. Imagine the energy draining off into the center of the earth. Washing your hands in cool water has the same effect, as water is a neutralizer.

The exercises are grouped according to ideas, so you can practice them in whatever sequence you wish. The only prerequisite is the relaxing and deepening. In fact, you may want to skip some of them completely and concentrate more fully on others, adapting them to your own needs. It is important to remember that each of us learns in ways that are unique. What is easy for one may be difficult for another. At all times it is important to go at your own pace and to use those exercises that make the most sense to you. You may find yourself adapting the exercises or altering them or even inventing ones of your own.

I hope these discoveries (my own and those of friends) will serve you well on the journey you are about to take. It is a journey that will expand your awareness of yourself far beyond your boundaries of ego to the multi-dimensions of the self. And it is a journey that has no end. To begin such a journey takes courage, for we are taught to think in terms of time and goals. The progress is sometimes slow and difficult. Yet it is a challenging journey, one that demands letting go of a known past and moving into an unknown future. It is commonly believed that any journey leading to greater self-awareness has perfection as its end result. This is a false assumption. While short-term goals may be an incentive to practice, the end of the journey is endlessness itself.

CHAPTER ONE

Deep Relaxation

To come to the dimension where you are open to receiving psychic and spiritual information and energy, you must first learn to relax and clear your body of tension. Total relaxation is a true gift, one which you need to learn to give yourself. It means that your body is completely loose, limp and relaxed and your mind is free and clear of all thoughts, fears and anxieties.

RELAXING YOUR BODY

There are many ways of moving into this relaxed state. For example, you might relax each body part in turn, beginning with your toes and moving up your body, or with your head and moving down. You may alternately tense and relax each body part. You may use an image that suggests an inward and downward movement (floating down a long, winding staircase, sailing on a boat, walking down a hillside). You may also use images that suggest inward and upward movements (floating, flying, climbing up a mountain, riding on a winged horse) since the result is the same. You may suggest to yourself that you will relax and deepen when focusing on a certain symbol: a flickering candle, a falling leaf, rolling waves. You may use colors, numbers or sounds. You may focus your awareness on your breathing, slowing and deepening the breath. Any of these methods will help you move into an altered state of consciousness.

This state, different from your usual waking reality, is a trance. It is a place of heightened awareness, an expansion of consciousness, and is not necessarily hazy or dreamlike. A trance is simply a very relaxed state of mind in which you are able to come in closer touch with your intuitive powers, images, symbols and feelings.

The light trance state is the same as the alpha dimension where the brain waves are slowed to the rate of fourteen impulses per second. There are many levels deeper than alpha in the trance state and you may feel yourself moving or changing levels. To work psychically, it is not necessary that you move into the deepest level of trance. The state you move into depends on how easily you relax and what is going on at the particular time. Like all skills, it will take some degree of practice to accomplish.

I'm often asked, "How do I really know I'm in a trance state?" There are certain bodily sensations you will come to recognize. Often you feel as though you are in a pre-sleep state—you are aware of what is happening around you, but only dimly. You are more in touch with your images and intuitions. Sometimes while in a trance you will feel your eyelids fluttering: you are experiencing REM, rapid eye movement, which also happens while you are dreaming. Sometimes your body will feel very light, or perhaps you will have no awareness of your body at all. At other times your body will feel so heavy that you could not possibly move it, or, you may experience the sensations of becoming either very large or very small. When you return to your normal awareness, you will realize that you have been someplace else.

RELAXING YOUR MIND

Once your physical body is relaxed, it is necessary to relax your mind and let go of thoughts and worries. Several images can help you clear your mind.

See before you an old black trunk with leather hinges and brass handles. Raise the lid of the trunk and place into it all your worries, fears, angers, pain and sorrow. Close the lid of the trunk. Your mind is now free.

See before you a huge tent filled with people, objects and feelings. As you concentrate on this tent, a sudden gust of wind blows through and sweeps the tent free of all clutter. Your mind is now as clear as that tent.

See before you a huge black cauldron and watch the flames swirl and dance above it. Gradually let the flames flicker and die until only the ashes remain. A sudden gust of wind blows the ashes away. The inside of the cauldron is clean. You notice it has a warm golden tone. As you focus on that soft golden glow, you too become golden.

See before you two beautiful butterflies. As you gaze on these butterflies, you are giving yourself wings, the ability to travel between dimensions.

As you focus on these images and only these images, you will gradually let go of your thoughts. If you have trouble keeping an image, just bring your consciousness back to the image each time it leaves, rather than trying to push the thoughts away.

2

CENTERING

When you are relaxed and your mind is clear, you can center your awareness. You may do this by breathing slowly and then, as you exhale, imagining that you are exhaling through a spot an inch or so below your navel. This is one of your *chakras* (see Chapter Three). Many of the martial arts use this energy center as a focal point for grounding the self. You may want to place your hand on your belly to help keep your focus there.

You may also center yourself by repeating the word "center" or by using a special number or color that brings you to a centering point. Another way to ground yourself is through the use of images. Imagine that you can extend your energy body deep into the center of the earth. Visualize slender ropes or roots extending from the base of your spine deep into the earth. This particular grounding technique is excellent to use before healing.

Breath awareness is another essential way of relaxing and centering. The human breath is the life force ebbing and flowing throughout the physical body. The ability to control the breath is the ability to control one's life force or vibration. As the breath changes, so does the vibration. Slower, deeper breathing moves you into a calmer, more centered space. Once this control is achieved, you will no longer be at the mercy of your emotions or your environment.

You will flow naturally when you can bring your own breath into harmony with the great breath—that is, the rhythm of the universe. There are many different ways of breathing, each having a specific purpose. What is important is learning to use the proper breath at the appropriate time.

Slow, deep breathing is necessary for moving into the trance state. It can be done in different ways. Experiment with it. Make sure you have enough ventilation in the room, and take care that you don't jump up too rapidly after the exercise. Most people are used to shallow breathing and the increase in oxygen when you fully inflate your lungs could make you feel dizzy.

One technique is pause breathing in which the length of the inhalation and exhalation are the same. The pause follows the exhalation rather than occurring between the inhalation and the exhalation as it usually does. Changing the pause focuses your awareness on your breath and brings you automatically to a calmer space. Keeping the inhalation and the exhalation the same regulates the breath and creates a space of inner balance. As you continue, try to lengthen the inhalations and exhalations. Inhale slowly through your nose; exhale slowly slowly through your nose, and pause. During the pause you will become more in touch with the sensations in your body. Hold the pause as long as it's comfortable for you. When you are used to breathing in this way, try to keep the pause the same length as the inhalation and exhalation.

Another technique is to lengthen the exhalations. You may do this by exhaling through your mouth as if you were blowing out a candle. You can also lengthen the exhalation by exhaling through your nose twice the count of the inhalation.

You may also deepen the breath by pausing twice. Inhale slowly through your nose, hold the breath, exhale slowly through your nose and pause again. Continue breathing in the same manner.

A fourth technique is to inhale slowly through your nose, hold the breath as long as it is comfortable for you and then exhale slowly through your nose.

One last technique: inhale slowly through your nose to the count of four, hold the breath to the count of twelve and exhale slowly to the count of eight. Any of these techniques will bring you into the meditative or trance state.

You are now able to relax, deepen and center. If you wish to deepen further after breathing rhythmically, you may count from ten to one. By the time you reach the count of one you will be more deeply in trance. Another method I use frequently for deepening is tracing my name in the sand and watching the waves wash it away. I continue tracing my name for a minute or two until I feel I have been carried as deeply as I wish. A third technique is to imagine yourself wandering down a hillside through a rainbow of colors. Each color carries you deeper. Begin with red, orange, yellow, green, blue, indigo and violet. I love this rainbow image because the rainbow is the path the Goddess Iris travels as she moves between heaven and earth.

USING A CIRCLE OF PROTECTION

The next step is the circle of protection. Use a circle any time you are doing psychic work. This is a precaution you must take when you open your mind. Just as you wouldn't open your door to strangers, you wouldn't want to open your mind to whatever happens to be around.

This circle is composed of anything that suggests protection to you. It may be light, color or sound vibrations, crystals, mirrors, or semi-permeable membranes. You may also use a comforting image. White light is considered good for general protection. Silver light is good for reflecting back any energy that you don't wish to absorb. (Be sure you imagine the energy dissipating harmlessly into the universe.) You may even imagine that you are dressing yourself in silver from head to toe. Be as creative as you wish with your protective circles. Try wrapping yourself in a rainbow: not only will you be fully protected but you will feel your spirits lifting. Use reds, oranges and yellows on cold days and blues and greens when the temperature rises.

Surrounding yourself with a circle of light allows you to remain receptive and open without absorbing any negative energy. It's a good idea to use a circle if you are with a friend who is depressed and you don't want to pick up any of her negativity. You will find that as your sensitivity increases, so will your need for protection.

Circles of protection can be used to protect things on the material plane such as your house, car or friends. What you are doing is increasing the energy of the force field or aura that naturally surrounds all things.

Circles protect in concrete, visible ways. One afternoon before leaving my apartment I circled it as usual. Later that night I returned to find a water pipe had broken and the hallway was filled with water. It had not yet begun to go under my front door. When I checked the basement, water had leaked on things people stored there but my things were unharmed. Another time while on vacation in the Canadian provinces I circled my car. When we returned I forgot to use the daily circle. That same day the line to the gas pedal broke. Fortunately I was close to home. While those instances may seem like coincidences at first, each new "coincidence" is harder to label this way.

When first using circles, you may wish to deepen slightly. Then see the circle and affirm to yourself, "This circle protects me from all harm." As you continue to work psychically you will not have to deepen before using the circles. You can recreate the circle whenever you feel the need.

If, for any reason, you feel the need for stronger protection you can use this technique. Light three white candles and sit or lie down with the candles spaced about twelve inches around you. Now relax, deepen and center yourself. Affirm to yourself: "I call upon the powers of the universe, all that is kind, loving and good. I call especially on my spirit guides to be with me and add their energy to mine. I am surrounding myself with a beautiful circle of light, a shimmering white light. This light protects me from all negativity. Nothing can harm me now, and this is true. I now release all negative energy from myself." Breathe deeply and exhale through your mouth as if you were blowing out a candle.

You may also protect yourself by telling yourself while in the trance state that whenever you say the word "circle" you will automatically be protected. Once you have talked to yourself several times, you can begin to use this technique. The more you use it, the better it works.

CREATING A PLEASANT MIND SPACE

You are now relaxed, deepened, centered and protected. The next step is the creation of a pleasant mind space in which you can do your psychic and creative work. You can create a mind space anytime you want to turn away from the outer world and tune into the inner world. Here are some beautiful and serene spaces I have used.

Walk down a long winding staircase that leads to a river where a small boat is tied. Sail off in the boat, floating down the river until your boat washes ashore at the edge of a meadow.

Fly on the back of a beautiful bird and land on the top of a mountain.

Ride a winged horse across the desert until you come to a cool oasis.

Ride in a crescent boat through a long, winding tunnel and come to rest in a quiet grotto.

Climb a long, winding path until you reach a cabin on the top of a mountain.

Walk through a cool, damp forest to a clearing where you rest beside a gurgling spring.

Enter a cave in the side of a hill and wander down through the labyrinth of time until you reach a healing space, a calm space.

The mind space is yours: you have created it. Use it whenever and however you wish. Meet your spirit guides there. Go to your space whenever you need healing. Communicate with your ideal or higher self. Use the space to solve your problems creatively. Heal and strengthen yourself by using affirmations. Re-enter your dreams and talk with the characters in your dreams. Go to the space and practice thought projection and creative visualization. (Each of these uses will be explained fully in later chapters.)

The following is a sample exercise for relaxing, centering and creating a mind space. All exercises will begin by saying "relax, deepen and protect yourself."

Relaxation Exercise

Lie down comfortably now, close your eyes and begin to relax. Let your body relax now. Allow yourself to become more and more relaxed. Breathe very deeply now and send your breath into your toes and feet. And let your breath like a healing massage break up any strain or tension and as you exhale let the tension drain away. Breathe deeply now and send your breath into your ankles and let your breath like a healing massage break up any strain or tension there and as you exhale let the tension drain away. Breathe deeply now and send your breath into your knees and let it break up any strain or tension there and as you exhale let the tension drain away. Breathe now into your thighs; your breath as a healing massage is breaking up any strain or tension and as you exhale the tension is draining away. Breathe into your genitals now; the deep relaxing energy is flowing into your genitals and any tension is draining away. Breathe into your buttocks; your breath as a healing massage is breaking up any strain or tension and as you exhale the tension is draining away. Breathe into your abdomen now; all your internal organs are soothed and relaxed and any strain or tension is draining away. Let your breath flow into your chest and breasts; let it soothe you and as you exhale any tension is draining away. Breathe into your back now; your breath like a healing massage is breaking up any strain or tension and as you exhale the tension is draining away. The deep relaxing energy is flowing through your back, into each vertebra as each vertebra assumes its proper alignment. And the healing breath is flowing into all your muscles and tendons and you are relaxed, very fully relaxed. Breathe into your shoulders and neck; your breath like a healing massage is breaking up any strain or tension and as you exhale the tension is draining away. Your shoulders and neck are fully relaxed. And the deep relaxing energy is flowing into your arms; your upper arms, your elbows, your forearms, your wrists, your hands, your fingers are fully relaxed. Breathe into your shoulders and neck again and let them relax. Become more and more relaxed. And let that relaxing energy wash up over your throat, and your lips, your jaw, your cheeks are fully relaxed. As you breathe into your face, the muscles around your eyes, your forehead, your scalp are relaxed. Any strain or tension is draining away. You are relaxed, most completely relaxed.

Picture three slender trees, three slender trees dancing in the wind. And as you focus on these trees, you become like the trees, firmly grounded. You have given yourself roots. You are safely grounded.

And let your mind clear, let it become relaxed and clear. Picture two beautiful butterflies. And as you focus on these butterflies, you become like the butterflies, light and free. And you have given yourself wings, wings to travel between dimensions. And now you have roots and wings.

To come to the dimension where you have access to psychic and spiritual information and energy, picture a black cauldron. And as you watch this huge black cauldron, the flames dance higher and higher. The warm, thick smoke curls upward. And slowly the flames grow smaller and dimmer, the flames flicker and die. And only the ashes remain. Suddenly a gust of wind blows through, sweeping the cauldron clean. And you notice that the inside has a warm and golden tone. Soft and golden. And as you gaze inward you are bathed in that golden glow and you are golden and protected from all harm.

And now float to your space, move between dimensions and travel to your space, a meadow, a mountain, a forest, the seashore, wherever your mind is safe and free. Go to that space now. And you are in your space, the space you have created, a space sacred and apart. And here in this inner world you are developing your natural psychic and healing abilities. Here in this space you are free from all tension and in touch with the calm, expansive power within you. Here in this space you are in touch with your body and able to heal whatever is wrong with you. Here in this space you have access to psychic and spiritual information and energy. Here is the space where you can communicate with your Oversoul, your spirit guides. Your flow is in harmony with the flow of the universe. Because you are a part of the whole creation you have access to the power of the whole of creation. Here you are pure and free.

Stay in this space a while and when you are ready let yourself drift up and back to your usual waking reality. *Pause about two minutes.* You will return relaxed, refreshed and filled with energy. And you will return now, gently and easily. Open your eyes and stretch your body.

CHAPTER TWO

Getting Clear

To have access to psychic and spiritual information, you must become a clear channel. This involves setting aside your personal thoughts, feelings, beliefs and experiences, as well as any unconscious fears, desires and anxieties. It is probably the hardest work you will do. Psychic information is available to everyone, but you have to be clear to receive it.

Sometimes your personal feelings can get in the way of your ability to perceive psychic information accurately. How can you learn to put aside your emotions and beliefs so that you are sure that what you are picking up is from a universal source and not your personal unconscious? As you grow to understand yourself, you won't be caught off guard when some of this unconscious material rises to the surface. Having worked so hard to acknowledge the existence of your feelings, it's important to realize that you are putting them aside only temporarily in order for you to work psychically. You are not repressing them.

Reflections and *Tidal Pools* are two guided fantasies that encourage you to observe yourself in non-judgmental ways. Most of us, having been raised in an atmosphere of criticism and competition, find it hard to really look at ourselves—after all, we might not like what we see. These exercises do not require you to change anything about yourself, only to notice yourself. They are intended to stimulate self-awareness, the realization that you are multi-dimensional. Some dimensions of yourself are joyful, exciting and likable, and others are not; but it is all you.

Sourcewaters of Woman has a different focus. It is a fantasy which enables you to reach your inner source of creativity and originality. I have often used this fantasy before beginning to write and it has proven an excellent stimulus.

With *Seasons* you can get in touch with your female cyclical nature. Your energy, like that of the universe, continually waxes and wanes. As you move with your own energy flow, you will become able to bring that flow into harmony with the flow of the universal energy.

With *Higher Self* you can contact your ideal self, your greater consciousness that has always existed. The higher self, also known as the Oversoul, exists on the astral plane, and by learning to contact it you will have knowledge and awareness not ordinarily accessible to you in your usual waking reality. You can meet this self through dreams, meditation and guided fantasy.

This higher self could also be called the voice of the soul. It is not to be confused with inner ego voices, those internalized parental and other authoritative voices. The voice of the soul speaks in loving ways and not in "shoulds." The inner voice is often denied in a society which places heavy emphasis on external authority. Children are taught not to trust themselves and are told that there is always someone else older, wiser, or stronger than they are.

It will take a certain amount of practice in clearing yourself before you can get in touch with the higher self. Practice deepening and centering, some simple healing and creative visualizations first. Remember, if you try it twice and aren't successful it means only that you need to practice more. Leave this exercise and try others before coming back to it. Patience is important. You can't play the piano after two lessons. So trust yourself and move at an easy, comfortable pace.

Reflections

Relax, deepen and protect yourself. And now go to a meadow. Easily float down or simply find yourself in a meadow, alone on a warm summer day. A gentle breeze is blowing and you walk through the meadow enjoying the warmth of the sun and the breezes on your body. Feel the grass brushing against your legs and smell the honeysuckle and the clover. Hear the song of the birds and feel a sense of oneness, a unity with all that is.

After walking a while you come now to a lake, a small, quiet lake. And you come to rest by that lake. Resting by the lake you gaze across the clear, blue water. And there in that water you see reflected an image, your face, your image mirrored in that lake. And as you watch your reflection it begins to move and change. And each movement, each subtle change suggests another dimension of your personality, another aspect of you, the you that existed before the you that now has your name. Watch the changing reflections. Watch and learn. Each change is but another part of you. *Pause about five or ten minutes.*

And now become aware of my voice again, calling you back from that lake, back through the meadow. Return easily to this room, bringing with you a new awareness of yourself and your many dimensions. Return wide awake and filled with energy. Open your eyes and stretch your body.

Tidal Pools

Relax, deepen and protect yourself. As you move deeper and deeper, letting yourself be carried very deeply into the realm of intuitions, images and imagination, come to a deserted beach and begin tracing your name in the sand and watching the waves wash it away until you have been carried as deeply as you wish. *Pause about two minutes.*

Still on that lovely, sunny beach you begin to wander slowly along the jagged shoreline, listening to the sound of the waves washing against the sand, smelling the salty sea air, hearing the cry of a gull and feeling the warmth of the sun on your body, aware of a growing sense of serenity and peace, a knowledge that all is one and you are one with all that is. *Pause about one minute.*

Now you come to rest beside a beautiful tidal pool. Here the water is very shallow and still. You watch the coral and the lovely sea anemones.

As you lean closer to the pool you see reflected there an image of yourself, a self that has many dimensions, a self that can be loving and kind, hateful and cruel, caring and indifferent, angry and peaceful, joyous and sad, weak and strong. Here in this space out of time you see yourself reflected and that reflection mirrors all that is you. *Pause about two minutes.*

Looking closer still you begin to focus on your limitations, your weaknesses. You see those attitudes and behaviors you would like to change. You see where your energy is blocked, places where you are hurt and scared, lonely and sad. You notice and accept all of this, secure in the knowledge that you are a strong person. *Pause about two minutes.*

Now reach your hands into the water and begin splashing, harder and harder. As you splash the images are dissolving, dissolving.

Now the water is still once again, crystal clear and very still. Once again you lean over the pool and see your reflection and mirrored there are all your strengths. See the places where your energy flows clearly and uninterruptedly. See your skills and sensitivities, your joys and successes. See those attitudes and behaviors that are rewarding and bring you peace and contentment. See the ways in which you wish to be *and you are,* simply by your intentions. *Pause about two minutes.*

Now to your surprise the pool has grown larger and deeper, so deep that you are able to dive right in, and that is what you do. Dive into the pool and merge with your powerful self, knowing that this is your power, the power to create, the power to imagine. This imagination is the goddess essence flowing through you. *Pause about two minutes.*

Now merged with your powerful self, rise up out of the water, out of the trance and return awake and refreshed to your waking reality. Open your eyes and stretch your body.

Reflections and *Tidal Pools* are two exercises you may want to do with a friend who can guide you. You know yourself, and if you feel that there is any chance something painful might be stimulated through these or other exercises, you might feel safer with a guide. Choose someone you trust who is confident that she will be able to move you out of a painful experience if that becomes necessary. To move someone out of a difficult experience you can say: "The image is quickly leaving; it has dissolved and you are safe, secure and relaxed." You may want to say: "I'm going to count from five to one and by the time I reach the count of one the image and any feelings connected with it will be gone and this is true." Then count. If necessary repeat the count. Even if you feel that you have come out of the trance, it is still a good idea to have your friend give the suggestion that the image and feelings connected with it have left.

You may also adapt the exercises and use only the part where you merge with your powerful self. This is an excellent way of lifting your spirits and reminding yourself of your positive attributes. You can also use this image to merge with a powerful trait that you have not yet developed. See yourself possessing the trait and then merge with that self. Using your imagination in this way, you are creating an inner change which will eventually manifest in your waking reality.

Sourcewaters of Woman

Relax, deepen and protect yourself. And now find yourself in a forest, a cool, dark forest. And this forest has a strange, magical quality. You are wandering alone, there is no sound, save the occasional crunch of the underbrush and your own gentle breathing. Here and there the darkness is dissolved by patches of sunlight creating dancing patterns as it filters through the trees.

Suddenly you come upon a small clearing. And here in the midst of the clearing is a natural bubbling spring. Eagerly you kneel beside the spring and taste the delicious water. As you lean over the spring and sip the clear, cool water you feel your consciousness being drawn down, down and down, your consciousness being drawn deep into the sourcewaters of woman.

Reach down now, still further down into that eternal source of womanwater, the spring that is as deep and deeper than your needs. "There will be no disappointment. Womanwater, emerald in motion, color clean and green as a leaf, as you love her wet beauty, the beauty of the water, you will also love yourself."* *Pause about two minutes.*

Consciousness swirling and deepening, reaching down, deeper down into the sourcewaters; here you will hear all of your voices as they empty into a rush of womanwater. These are the voices of your creativity springing from your soul, your psyche, the deepest center of your originality. *Pause about five minutes.*

Reaching still deeper, deeper and deeper, dipping deeply into your creativity, your voices, your visions, taking from them as you will, knowing that the source is eternal. *Pause about five minutes.*

Now the voices are fading, the visions are fading. Your consciousness is swirling and rising, moving up and back, swirling

*Adapted from Sue Silvermarie, "River at Nantasket," in *Letters of a Midwife* (Milwaukee, Wisconsin, 1975).

13

around and up to your usual waking reality. Return and bring with you some of those visions and voices. Return now and be wide awake and filled with energy. Open your eyes and stretch your body.

Seasons

Relax, deepen and protect yourself. As woman, you are in touch with the cycles of nature, intimately connected with the ebb and flow of the tides, the waxing and waning of the moon. Knowing of earth and matter, you will move deeper and deeper within. Move so deeply within that you will experience all of the rhythms and cycles of nature as they occur on the planet earth.

You will experience the coming and passing of the seasons: the harmony and direction, the spontaneity and the consistency, the continually rearranging balance. And you will feel them in ways that are at once universal and personal.

Now it is spring and Persephone's return, the earth swells with the joyful reunion. There is an awakening, a new awareness, the joyous expectancy of new life. *Pause about three minutes.*

Now the summer, the ripening, the coming harvest, the season of the corn mothers, the sultry sensuousness of the summer. *Pause about three minutes.*

Now the fall, the harvest. The days are growing shorter and cooler. *Pause about three minutes.*

Now the winter, the goddess dons her wintry robes. The decay and dying, the cold and dying. Knowing your own dying. *Pause about three minutes.*

Once again spring, the rebirth, the joy and the realization that life continues. Feel this continual ebb and flow within, knowing that you are maiden, mother and crone. *Pause about three minutes.*

Now let your energy gently ebb and flow, moving you up and back to your waking reality. And you are wide awake and filled with energy. Open your eyes and stretch your body.

Higher Self

Relax, deepen and protect yourself. And now move even deeper, move very deeply within. I am going to count from ten to one and by the time I reach the count of one you will be deep, very, very deep. *Count.*

You are now very deeply in trance, you are now moving into your greater awareness, into your higher self. Feel your consciousness expanding. You are very light and very free, growing, glowing, expanding, moving easily into your greater awareness, into your goddess essence. And from this greater perspective, you will have knowledge and experience not ordinarily accessible to you in your usual waking reality.

You may now look at your life as you form it. You will become aware of yourself, your soul's purposes, and you will be able to integrate this knowledge and awareness into your usual waking reality. Stay with this perspective now and observe your life in a loving and spontaneous way. *Pause about five or ten minutes.*

Now feel this awareness fading as you move up and back into your waking reality, bringing with you all that you have gained. Know that you can come into contact with this aspect of yourself whenever you wish. And now open your eyes and be filled with energy.

Doing trance work often makes feelings very accessible. Once you allow yourself to relax, any feelings that have been repressed or denied tend to surface, often with an uncomfortable intensity. When this happens, continue to let the feelings surface. They will flow through you if you allow them to. Notice the sensations in your body as the feelings emerge. Notice any words or pictures that form in your mind. Go with them. Follow the pictures in your mind's eye as though you were watching a play. Remember, you are not a critic, simply an observer. Continue to notice all the feelings that arise, and accept them as they flow through you. Releasing feelings is a continuous process that begins with the acknowledgement of the feelings.

You must realize how you feel and then learn to accept it. This does not mean that you hang on to the feeling, only that you admit they are your own. Then you can release them. There are certain feelings (anger, for example) that are unacceptable to many people. This makes it harder to recognize and accept such feelings. Choose the feeling you wish to examine— in this case, anger. Now relax, deepen and protect yourself. Go to your mind space and ask yourself about anger. Do you ever feel angry? What makes you angry? How do you express your anger? By shouting, withdrawing, sarcasm, self-pity, etc.? What are your fears about expressing anger? How was anger treated in your family? What are your beliefs about anger? Do you think it is evil, destructive, uncivilized, etc.? Now recall an incident in which you became angry. Where did it take place and who was involved? Did you realize your anger immediately or much later? Did you express it? How? Notice if there is anything similar about the times, places or people that make you angry. Now erase those images and imagine yourself in a new situation in which you become angry. Allow yourself to express the anger without censoring your behavior. Now let those images go and return to your usual awareness.

If you expressed your anger in a way that you consider inappropriate— for example, if you overreacted and said things that you would later regret— you have now become aware of it. Try not to criticize yourself, only to acknowledge that you have the right to become angry and you are going to learn to express it in an appropriate way. On the psychic level you can use affirmations to help learn this. One such affirmation might be, "I am able to express my anger openly and directly."

You can also use the trance state to imagine yourself expressing anger appropriately. To do this, relax, deepen and protect yourself. Then imagine that you are expressing your anger in an appropriate way. For example, visualize yourself saying to your roommate: "It makes me angry when you leave your dirty dishes. Please clean up after yourself." Visualize this for several minutes and then return to your usual reality. This technique, called "creative visualization," is an excellent way of working to change behavior patterns.

It takes time to learn self acceptance and to be able to express feelings honestly and directly. You will be able to act spontaneously only to the extent that you trust yourself and know that you are responding to the present situation and not bringing with you any unconscious, repressed feelings. Once you can act in this way, you will no longer be controlled by your feelings. You will be aware and you will accept them, thus choosing when and how to express them appropriately.

Your feelings are not you; they are your physical and mental responses to people and situations. These feelings should be allowed to flow through you. If you cling to feelings or repress them, they build up and block your free-flowing energy.

Fear is the root of all negative emotions. Greed, envy, hatred—all stem from fear. The opposite of fear is love. Love is the constant all-pervasive force which binds the universe together. The less fearful you become, the greater your ability to give and receive love. When you love, when you allow the universal force to flow through you in an unforced way, you become forceful and powerful. When you understand and flow with this universal energy, you can truly give without forcing yourself on someone, and you can also receive without becoming greedy.

It is often said that a little fear is a good thing: if you weren't afraid of getting hit by a car, you wouldn't look before crossing the street. What is really needed is *caution,* not fear. It makes good sense to be cautious, to become aware of your surroundings. It does not make good sense to become afraid. Fear causes you to tense and your energy becomes blocked. Letting go of fear does not mean letting go of good sense. It doesn't mean that you walk head on into a truck because you no longer fear it: you must be aware of your limitations. If you see a wall in front of you, you can walk around it, climb over it or crawl under it. But you can't walk through it, at least not in your physical body.

You can use the trance state to help release your fears. To accomplish this, relax, deepen and protect yourself. Then go to your mind space. While in this space ask yourself, "What am I afraid of?" and let the images arise. Conjure up the images clearly, and vividly experience them, acknowledging those fears that are within you. Then slowly dissolve the images by either erasing them (use a giant eraser if you wish) or transform them into loving friendly images, for example change a raging lion into a gentle kitten. (Remember, we are dealing with the symbolic transformation of fearful images. I am not suggesting that if a lion is actually attacking you that you close your eyes and pretend it is a kitten.) Now affirm that the fear has been transformed, and you will no longer be affected by it in any way that is detrimental to you.

Another exercise to aid in releasing fears and painful experiences is *Letting Go.* You can use this exercise to erase an hour's, day's or week's experiences. If you have had a very traumatic experience, you may need to work on it on several different occasions. It will take as long as it takes. You may need to repeat the exercise once, twice or many times. Each time you do the exercise, you are releasing more pain and becoming clearer. Every-

17

one has regrets and painful experiences, but it is not necessary to continue to carry them. This exercise can be done alone, or you may wish to choose a trusted friend to guide you.

Letting Go

Relax, deepen and protect yourself. Travel easily to a safe mind space. Here in this space you can recreate your day, a day that has been difficult for you. Conjure up each thought, each act, each word that you regret. See them all very clearly. *Pause about three to five minutes.*

Now take the images one at a time and watch as they grow smaller, smaller and smaller. Help the images grow smaller. They are dissolving, growing smaller and fainter until they no longer exist. This image no longer has the power to hurt or disturb you in any way. It is dissolved, washed away, completely erased.

And now conjure up each word, each act, each thought that you enjoyed, that you consider important, anything that you feel positive about. Conjure up each happy thought, fleeting smile, pleasant experience. And let these images grow. Let them become larger and larger. Let them spill over into your consciousness. You are bathed in the joy of the remembered experience. *Pause about three to five minutes.*

These positive experiences will continue to grow and develop. They will remain a part of you always. Swim in these images now, remembering, recreating and rejoicing in them. They will remain a part of you now and always.

And now when you are ready, you may return to your usual awareness, released of all pain and fear and filled with a joyful and loving energy. Take your time. Then open your eyes and stretch your body.

Three images that I use to let go of feelings and release blocked energy are: *Whirlpool, Waterfall, and Shedding the Cloak of Negativity.*

Whirlpool

Relax, deepen and protect yourself. Now imagine that you
have come upon a beautiful natural spring. You dip into that
water and find it warm and inviting. The water is not deep, only
up to your shoulders if you are sitting. And you do sit and relax
in that warm water. The water begins to bubble and swirl around
you. Swirling and whirling, the water churns over and around you.
And you feel your muscles relaxing, become more and more relaxed. The water is swirling and circling and you are letting go,
letting go of tension and pain. The water is washing away all that
anxiety, all that fear. And the warmth and the movement of the
water is soothing and relaxing you. And you are releasing all that
tension. Let the swirling waters soothe and heal you. And when
you are ready swim up and back to your usual waking reality.
And you will return relaxed, calm and centered.

Waterfall

Relax, deepen and protect yourself. And now find yourself at
the foot of a mountain. Begin that gradual ascent now and as you
wind your way slowly along that mountain path you become
aware of a heaviness, a tiredness, a sense of anger, futility or pain.
Your climb is slower and you realize those burdens that you are
carrying, burdens that you had not even realized you had asked
for, but that you are carrying nevertheless. And the sun grows
hotter as it climbs higher in the sky. And you travel on. Soon
you come to rest by a small crevice in the rocks and suddenly a
stream of water appears, and the stream widens, the water rushing
down the rocks. You shed your clothes and stand beneath that
waterfall. Feel the clear, cool water pouring down upon you. Let

that gentle stream of water wash away all your fears, all your sorrows, all your anxiety. *Pause about two minutes.*

Now stepping out from under the waterfall you rest for a while, letting yourself be dried by the sun. Let the sunlight stream down upon you and fill every cell and tissue until you feel light and refreshed and renewed. When you are ready you can return to your usual awareness, relaxed, refreshed and filled with energy.

Shedding the Cloak of Negativity

Relax, deepen and protect yourself. Here in this space out of time you are becoming conscious of the garment you are wearing, a cloak, a heavy, black cloak. This dark, hooded robe is the cloak of your negativity. It symbolizes all the negative thoughts, feelings and experiences you carry with you. Feel the heaviness of it. Become aware of the texture and the feel of the cloth. Feel the weight on your shoulders, your whole body cloaked in negativity and despair. *Pause about one minute.*

And now, become aware that the cloak is gradually lifting up and away from your body and with it your negativity and despair. Now the cloak has vanished.

And your attention is drawn to a fountain, a fountain of light, an incredible fountain of light. And the shimmering light is bubbling up and spilling over. A shower of light, shower of stars, thousands of tiny stars, is streaming down upon you. The whole space is filled with a brilliant light.

And you realize that you are gowned in a new garment, a sheer translucent cloak of light woven from the stars. And you are wearing this robe of love, joy and protection. It is the symbol of your womansoul, the loving connections you feel and sense and see. Wear it now and always. When you are ready, drift up and back to your waking reality filled with light and love.

MEDITATION

Meditation is a conscious activity in which you still the mind by stopping the flow of images and thoughts. It is a way of cleansing the mind of all fears and releasing new reservoirs of creativity and energy. In meditation you connect the personal self with the universal self. You bring your breath in harmony with the great breath. Each time you relax and become more centered, you move beyond the apparent duality of the cosmos.

Affirmations, *mantras*, breath control and awareness are all useful in meditation. Affirmations are positive statements, affirming your health, strength and wisdom, which are repeated over and over while in the trance state. *Mantras* are words or syllables whose rhythm and sound produce an altered state of consciousness. You begin by vocalizing the sound (chanting), and gradually the vocalization becomes mental and is repeated over and over in the mind. Breath control is achieved through specific breathing exercises as explained in Chapter One.

To meditate you must first develop your powers of concentration. Relax and deepen yourself by following the ebb and flow of your breath. Now focus all your attention on a single image such as a flickering candle. Actually burning a candle helps, but you may simply use the mind image. If you are using a burning candle, keep your attention on that candle for several minutes and then close your eyes and create that candle in your mind's eye. Imagine that the energy of the flame is flickering in you. Become aware of your own energy, burning brightly like the candle, an eternal flame. If any other thoughts arise, turn away from them and bring your attention back to the candle.

It may take awhile before you are able to concentrate in this way. Even if you feel it isn't working, continue to take several minutes a day to practice. If you are able to choose the same time each day, it is even better because you are establishing that habit in your mind. In the beginning, attempt it only for a short time, about three to five minutes. In order for a habit to grow and develop, you need to go at a pace that's comfortable for you. Once you have established the habit and can concentrate successfully, you will automatically lengthen your time. If you begin by trying to set twenty or thirty minutes aside, you may think that you really can't take that amount of time every day and the habit may fall by the wayside.

When practicing meditation, sit in a comfortable position with your back as straight as possible. You may sit in a chair with your feet firmly on the floor or sit on the floor. Your legs may be crossed or outstretched. It is not necessary to sit in the lotus or half lotus position to meditate. Easterners learned that position long ago because it was comfortable for them. They had no chairs, and in the cross-legged or lotus position they felt balanced and could keep their spines straight. You can meditate just as success-fully in any other position as long as you are comfortable and try to keep your spine as straight as you can. You may want to try tucking your chin in slightly and focusing your awareness on the point between your eyebrows known as the third eye. This is your intuitive center, the space where con-scious and unconscious knowledge join.

You are now sitting in a meditative position. Relax yourself and take a few deep breaths. Now choose an image, affirmation or *mantra* and repeat it over and over in your mind. Focus only on that and nothing else. If your thoughts wander, bring them back to your chosen focus. After about five to fifteen minutes return to your usual awareness. Give yourself time to return slowly. Don't leap up, it could make you feel dizzy.

Several images that I have found useful are a flickering candle, a single rose, a quiet lake, the ocean waves, a shower of stars, moonbeams across the water, a mountain top. One of my favorite meditations is the color med-itation in which I visualize in turn all the colors of the rainbow—red, orange, yellow, green, blue, indigo and violet. When I reach violet I dissolve the colors and begin again. Sometimes I draw the colors up through the *chakras* (see Chapter Three): beginning with the root *chakra,* I draw in the color red and continue until I reach the crown *chakra* drawing in violet. Then I begin again.

At other times I meditate by focusing my awareness on my breathing and the sensations in my body. When I do breath awareness meditation I meditate about twenty to sixty minutes. This kind of meditation is very grounding because it keeps your attention focused on your body and on the present moment. If the mind wanders, it can be brought back to the breathing.

I focus on my breathing, paying attention to the quality and length of my breath, and watch the path it takes as the air enters my nostrils and moves down the back of my throat and into my lungs and diaphragm. I then let my consciousness encircle my body, starting with my head, and I become very attentive to the movements and changes within. As I go deep-er, I become aware of the more subtle bodily changes and motions.

Clear and concentrated attention on the breath will give you insights into your behavior. For example, do you cling to the inhalation or struggle to push and release the exhalation? In your daily life are you troubled by clinging attitudes or do you exhaust yourself with struggles to release, to experience more, to continually move on? How does your mind play tricks on you? Does your attention wander? Are you holding on to the past or escaping into the future? Does your mind race or do you become sleepy and lethargic? What feelings come up? Sometimes it will be hard to sit with your feelings, but sitting *with* your feelings is not the same as sitting *on* them and repressing them.

Become aware of all these things during meditation. Don't try to change them, only become aware of them. With patient and continued practice you will realize that noticing is a way of accepting and centering the self.

Here are several affirmations that lend themselves easily to meditation. "All is one and I am one with all that is." "I have found the inner harmony that flows through me and my body and mind." "There is a golden spirit flowing through me and within that spirit I will live." "There is a harmony of season and direction." "I know I am where I'm supposed to be." "We all are one and the force that holds us together is love."

I sometimes use *mantras* that were taught to me by a friend who practices *Kundalina Yoga.* I have adapted or altered them slightly to fit my needs and beliefs. I enjoy the sound vibration and feel a great concentration of energy whenever I use them. It is not necessary to use these particular *mantras* to meditate; if they sound too mystical or alienating, just forget them. There are many other affirmations you can use.

The first *mantra* I used was the Tibetan *"Om mani padme hum."* *Om* is pronounced "aum" and is the symbolic sound of the infinite power or divine universe. *Mani* means jewel, which is our inner self. *Padme* means lotus flower, which is similar to the water lily and grows up out of the mud,

blooming when it reaches the surface of the water, each petal unfolding to reveal the innermost bloom. *Hum* is pronounced "hung" and symbolizes the vibrations of energy we send out. The entire *mantra* then symbolizes the give and take of energy. We breathe in the universal energy, work to let go of fear, envy and hate so that our true self shines forth and gives back our glowing vibration—thus the cycle is complete.

The next *mantra,* from *Kundalina Yoga,* is *"Sat nam."* As you meditate, inhale *Sat* and exhale *nam. Sat* means truth and *nam* is name. Truth is the essence of the infinite energy. This *mantra* may also be broken down into the individual sounds *"Sa ta na ma." Sa* is infinity, *ta* is birth, *na* is death, *ma* is rebirth. If you wish, you may incorporate hand movements with this *mantra.* Press the index finger to the thumb on *sa,* the middle finger to the thumb on *ta,* the ring finger to the thumb on *na* and the little finger to the thumb on *ma.* Continue this cycle making the movements with both hands simultaneously.

I begin my daily *yoga* practice with this *mantra: "Ong namo guru dev namo."* Its meaning, in essence, is "I call upon the divine teacher within." This *mantra* may be chanted out loud three times in this way: Take a deep breath and exhale *"ong namo"* on the same tone; take another short or half breath and exhale the last three words of the *mantra. Dev* is chanted one tone higher than *ong namo guru,* and the *namo* is the same tone as *ong.* I like this *mantra* because it centers me and affirms my inner wisdom. I sometimes repeat it before doing readings or other psychic work.

Another *mantra* that I chant out loud, also taken from *Kundalini Yoga* and adapted for my needs, is *"Ad such jugad such ebay such i hosibi such."* It means "God was true in the beginning, God has always been true, God is true now and I say that God will always be true." God is the name many people have given to the universal creative force. All life is composed of three principles or forms of energy—generating, organizing and destroying. Thus, most religions describe a triune god. When I personify this force I imagine a Goddess, a mythic woman whose attributes personify all that is strong, nurturing and loving in the universe.

The last *mantra* calls upon this divine mother. Sit comfortably in a meditative position. Cup your right hand over your ear with the palm on your cheek. Inhale deeply and exhale *ma.* The cupped hand will increase the vibration. Followers of *Kundalina Yoga* use this *mantra* in a special position. If you wish to try it and are flexible enough to do so, sit on the floor with your back straight. Now pull your right knee into your chest, keeping your foot on the floor. Bend your left knee to the side, touching or as close to the floor as you can with your left sole touching the side of your right foot. Place your right elbow on your right knee and cup your right hand over your right ear so that your palm is resting on your cheek bone. Make a fist with your left hand and raise your arm in the air. You are pulling in the universal energy with your left hand and sending out your own vibration through your right side. This creates the continual flow of energy. Take a deep breath and slowly exhale, letting your breath form the sound *ma.* Inhale deeply again and exhale the sound *ma.* Continue this for as long as you feel comfortable.

A *mantra* is a specific psychic technique for concentrating and focusing energies. It is not necessary to use any one *mantra.* Humming or chanting "woman" will also raise your vibration. Create your own special sounds to stimulate your energies. There are no secrets to this universal power. It is open to all. Meditation is a way of releasing fears and negativity. It improves your concentration and allows you to receive information from the unconscious. It is a way of connecting with the universal mind. It will take practice and patience to develop the ability to meditate. But with perseverance you will be able to clear your mind of all thoughts and fears and, in so doing, you will begin to live fully in the present.

Meditation enables you to develop the attitude of non-attachment. Nonattachment is not a withdrawal from life, but the ability to look in a loving way at your successes and failures, understanding the reasons for both. It is this inner peace that allows you to view your life, both its joys and tragedies, with a serene and composed attitude.

PRAYERS, BLESSINGS AND INVOCATIONS

Meditation stills the mind; you become open and receptive to all that is. In meditation you receive from the universe. Prayer, on the other hand, is the asking. In prayer we speak to the universe, we ask to harmonize our needs with the needs of all that is. We pray not only for ourselves but for all creatures. Prayers, blessings and invocations often flow through me. I have included them, not to be a part of a feminist liturgy, but as an acknowledgement of prayer as a part of my own spiritual practice.

Prayer

Blessed be thou Creatress of Life whose love forever shines within me. Help me to use thy energy to direct my force. Light my path that I may follow it in love, secure in the knowledge that I move from a source deep within me. Let me use my energy to create the world anew. Instill in me an awareness of the rhythms and cycles of nature so that I may intuitively know the time to build up and the time to tear down; the time to speak and the time to remain silent; the time to move and the time to stand still. Let me sense now and always the depth of our connections. For we are all one and the force that holds us together is love.

Group Blessing for Full Moon
Tonight is the night of the full moon
The night of Selene—wise and knowing
Tonight we connect with her power and it is ours.
Tonight we vibrate with the pulse of the moon
Knowing, sensing and feeling our connections
We flow in many dimensions.
Our eyes are opened and we see with clarity our visions
Our ears are opened and we hear the voices of our souls
Our mouths are opened and we speak with wisdom
Our hearts are opened and we are filled with love
Our wombs are opened and we are in touch with the source
  of our creativity
Our feet are opened and we walk on our own true path
Our hands are opened and our power is manifest.

Prayer
Let me sink deep within the source of creativity
Deep within my originality
Let me connect with all that is divine in me
My power to imagine, to create anew
Let me surrender now to the sea of my greater consciousness.

Prayer
Blessed be Oh Lady of the Waters
May I swim forever within thy embrace
Help me to see my true self mirrored in thy reflections
Encourage my energy to flow as surely as your tides
And know that the source is eternal, flowing, changing.

Prayer
Oh Lady of Silver Magic wise and knowing
Be with us as we open our hearts to thy comfort, wisdom and guidance.
Protect us now and always
Direct our footsteps on our own true path
That we may come to a deeper, richer understanding
  of each other and ourselves.

Prayer
Oh Great One
I see your beauty surrounding me—sky, earth, sea
I feel the warmth of your touch as the sun kisses my face

26

I hear the sound of your voice as the wind moves through
the trees
I smell your essence in the salty, sea air.
May I always feel your presence, the strength of our
connections
Let me live now and always within your embrace for I have
never been without you.

Invocation

Creature of fire let me unite with you that I may have
passion and power
Creature of water let me unite with you that I may have
fluid motion
Creature of air let me unite with you that I may have
wisdom and intuition
Creature of earth let me unite with you that I may have
stability and steadfastness.

CHAPTER THREE

Energy and Vibration

The universe is composed of whirling energy vibrating at different frequencies. The patterns and forms vary: some are matter and some vibrations. But it is all energy and can be neither created nor destroyed, only transformed. You are being bombarded by energy all the time, often without realizing it: radio waves, light waves, sound waves, x-rays. Forces of gravity pull down upon you, and the air continually presses against you.

Human beings are also energy forms, and as such emit waves of energy which respond to and interact with countless other waves of energy. The energy in your body and the energy in the universe are the same. Sometimes the energy expands and sometimes it contracts. The Chinese concept of yin and yang describes this inward and outward flow of energy. Yin (the female, the receptive) and yang (the male, the aggressive) are manifestations of the same energy. Both patterns are necessary for life: as in breathing, both the inhalation and the exhalation are essential. Without that continual flow, there could be no motion, no action, and therefore no life.

If you become too identified with one form of energy, you become unbalanced. The emphasis has usually been on the yang, the aggressive. The ideal balance is one that is continually rearranging itself, manifesting different qualities at different times.

The universal energy is always available to you: you have all the energy you need. If you fill your mind with fears and problems, you block the flow of energy. If you focus your mind on the universal energy, it will flow freely through you. The amount of energy available to you is in direct proportion to the universality of your motives. Each time you come from a space of fear, anger, greed or envy, you limit the flow of energy. Each time you are motivated by love and work towards the higher good, the energy available to you increases. In actuality, the energy of the universe is limitless and is diminished only by your fears and learned limitations. Each time you give out energy, new energy flows into its place. It is only when you try to hoard the energy that the vital force is restricted. This is sometimes referred to as the universal law of supply and demand. Here is an affirmation describing life's continual flow of energy. "All that I need is drawn to me. All that I have I give away. All that I give comes back to me—tenfold."

The following exercise gives practice in experiencing the continual flow of energy within the body.

Pitcher of Water

This exercise is done standing. Close your eyes and relax your body. Now imagine that you are a pitcher of water. Bend slowly to the right as you imagine the water pouring out. Bend only as far as you can without losing your balance. Now move slowly back to an upright position, imagining that the pitcher is again filling with water. Now bend slowly to the left as you imagine the water pouring out. Bend only as far as you can without losing your balance. Once again move back to an upright position. Repeat these motions several times until you feel comfortable doing them. Now begin to walk around the room, slowly and deliberately, using the same images. Lift your right foot and as you do imagine all the water flowing into your left side so that your right side is completely empty. Then place your right foot slowly down as you imagine all the water flowing into your right side. Bend as far as you can without losing your balance. When your left leg feels completely empty, lower it and continue the movements with your right leg. Keep moving around the room for several minutes using the image of emptying and filling. Now stop the movement while one leg is several inches off the ground, remain stationary for several seconds and then begin the movement again. Continue in this fashion for several minutes.

The physical body is but one manifestation of the total energy being. The energy bodies are not separate from the physical, but are vibrations that vary in frequency from the most dense (the physical) to the most subtle spiritual body. The energy bodies (also known as astral bodies) are less easily perceived and less limited than the physical body: they can change size, shape, density and intensity. At present, western scientists have been able to measure only a small part of the total energy: body heat, the electromagnetic field and the layer of ionized sweat surrounding the body.

Yet most of us are aware of another person's energy. Often if we feel tense, tired or relaxed when in the company of another person, it's because we are absorbing some of their energy. The next exercise will help you to become more consciously aware of someone else's energy.

Energy Exercise

Work with a partner. Stand facing her and center yourself. Allow your breath to become slow and deep. Inhale slowly through your nose and exhale slowly, again through your nose. Imagine that as you exhale your exhalation is flowing through your palms. Imagine the flow of breath as entering through your nose and leaving through your palms. Concentrate on this for several minutes. Notice any sensations you feel in your hands. Now extend your arms slightly so that your palms are close to your partner's palms but not touching. Tune into your partner's energy. Notice any sensations between your palms. As you become aware of the energy flowing between you and your partner, begin to separate. Move slowly apart, keeping your attention on your palms and the energy flowing from you and your partner. See how far apart you can move while still keeping the energy flowing between you.

Once aware of your own energy and the energy of others, you can share this energy, raise more energy or get in touch with the universal energy through the formation of an energy circle. An energy circle is formed when two or more women sit or stand in a circle holding hands. The vibrations of sound are particularly strong, so humming, chanting and singing are often used in the energy circle.

Building and sharing energy in this way is what the witches referred to as "raising the cone of power." This is a concentration of energy that, once raised, can be directed at will for healing or towards the fruition of some individual or group project.

Energy Circle

Sit in a circle holding hands. Hold the left palm up, since that is the side you will receive the energy from, and the right palm down, since that is the side you will send the energy from. Close your eyes and begin breathing slowly and deeply. Ground yourself by sending a portion of your energy body deep into the center of the earth. Then begin to bring your breathing together. Visualize the circle surrounded by healing, protective energy. See the energy as a pool of liquid light at your feet. As you inhale, draw the light up through the soles of your feet and feel it move slowly throughout your body. Pull it up through your legs and into your hips. Let it move slowly along your spine. Feel it move into your shoulders and neck, down your arms and into your hands, back up your shoulders and neck again. Draw the energy into your head and imagine it flowing out the top of your head, spilling over and around you. This is the energy of the universe, the energy of life. It is this energy that you are connecting with and this energy that you will send around the circle. Draw this energy now into your body by pulling it or simply letting it flow into your left hand, flow throughout your body and then let it flow out of your right hand to the woman on your right. Let yourself merge with the swirling, circling energy. Feel the magic; let it take you over.

After about ten minutes or longer, if you wish, you may end the circle by dropping your hands and opening your eyes. The circle may be ended with words such as "May the energy we shared here be with us while we are apart" or "The circle is open but not broken."

When first doing energy circles, you may feel more comfortable with a guide. The guide takes responsibility for beginning and ending the circle. She helps everyone to relax and focus and begin breathing together. She may start the energy flowing by pressing the hand of the woman on her right. As the woman receives the energy she sends it throughout her body and then out her right hand. As she sends the energy she will press the woman's hand on her right and each woman will do so, in turn, around the circle.

Other possibilities for energy circles are as follows:

1. The guide can mention each woman's name, beginning with the woman on her right and ending with herself, suggesting that loving energy be sent to each.

2. Each woman can mention herself.

3. Each woman, in turn, can enter the circle and receive the energy.

4. Names of those not present can be placed in the circle by naming them silently or out loud, and the energy can be sent to them.

5. Women can meditate on something of importance to the group, and energy can be directed toward it.

6. Each woman, in turn, can make a wish. All can meditate on it, sending energy to the wisher and visualizing her desire being fulfilled.

7. Affirmations such as "We are all one" can be used.

8. The women can hum, using the vibrations to build the energy. You may want to place your hands on the nape of the neck of the woman to your right, and so on around the circle.

9. Chant your own names in a round.

10. Chant the names of the Goddess in a round (Diana, Isis, Aphrodite, or any other Goddess's name).

11. Sing or chant appropriate words such as:

"We are women giving birth to ourselves, to ourselves
We are women giving birth to ourselves."

"Oh Divine Mother, Oh Divine Mother,
Oh Divine Mother, Oh Divine Mother."

"Mother, Daughter, Sister, Lover
Hear us, hear us
It is you we seek within us
Goddess, Goddess."

"Woman am I, Spirit am I
I am the infinite within my soul
I have no beginning, I have no end
All this I know." *

*Women's Oral Tradition

32

Animal Metamorphosis and *Body Awareness* are two beginning exercises which encourage the mind to explore and create new shapes and forms. I have included these exercises here because they are among the first exercises I teach in my classes and are a good preparation for more complex exercises, such as hand levitation and astral projection. In *Animal Metamorphosis* you fantasize your body changing into that of a cat and a bird and then you explore those sensations and feelings for a while. I have written the exercises separately, but they may both be done during the same trance. The *Body Awareness* exercise continues the transformation fantasy. This time your body assumes familiar shapes of nature: trees, rocks, stars, rain.

Animal Metamorphosis

Relax, deepen and protect yourself. And now you are moving down and down. And as you continue that downward and inward movement you feel that your body is moving and changing also. Changing very easily now, changing into the body of a cat. Feel your arms and legs changing into paws, your skin into fur, your face growing whiskers. And now in that cat's body allow yourself to move and stretch, to be stroked and rubbed. Move with a new found grace and agility and enjoy these movements a while. *Pause about two minutes.*

And now feel your body changing again, changing back into your usual body. Your own body and identity completely restored. Back into your own body now you will return to your usual consciousness, wide awake and filled with energy. Open your eyes and stretch your body.

* * *

Relax, deepen and protect yourself. You are deepening, moving inward and as you continue that inward movement you sense a change. Your body is changing. Your body is growing smaller and lighter and changing into that of a bird. Feel your arms changing into wings, your skin into feathers, your mouth into a beak and your feet into claws. And now in this graceful bird's body you begin to fly, to soar high above the earth. Enjoy these sensations and feelings for a while. *Pause about two minutes.*

33

And now feel your body changing again as you begin to resume your own form. Your own body and your own identity completely restored, you are back into your body and moving back to your usual awareness. Return wide awake and filled with energy. Open your eyes and stretch your body.

Body Awareness

Relax, deepen and protect yourself. And now listen to my words as they carry you deeper, deeper and deeper, to the realm where you can experience your body in any way that you wish. You are going deeper and deeper now and feeling very heavy. Your body is growing heavier and heavier, so heavy that you couldn't possibly move it. Feel that incredible heaviness, that weight that leaves you motionless.

Now that heaviness is leaving and your body is becoming lighter and lighter. So light that you are floating up in the air, floating, drifting, soaring, high above the earth now. You are effortlessly floating along, consciousness condensed to a tiny cell, a tiny cell floating off into the cosmos.

And now consciousness expands once again, expands and descends, down to earth. You are touching the earth again and feeling the richness of the earth beneath your feet, standing firmly on the earth, mother earth.

And now your body is changing, changing into a mountain rising high above the earth, a strong, high mountain.

The mountain is growing smaller now, smaller and smaller until you are a small rock. Feel what it is like to be that round rock with a hole in the center, symbolic of the Goddess Diana, conical-shaped rock, symbol of the first moon Goddess in a very dim past.

That rock is changing now into wood, feeling as wood, like a strong, energetic tree, offspring of mother earth, roots planted firmly in the ground, leaves rustling, swaying in the breeze.

And now you are becoming the breeze, a warm, gentle breeze. And now you are growing cooler and stronger, a cooling breeze bringing the rain. It is raining gently now, rain becoming heavier and heavier, pouring down upon the earth.

And the rain is stopping. The earth is dried by the sun and you are the sun, shining brightly. Daytime star, strong healing energy. And now sunlight is fading, day changing into night. You are Harmonia weaving the starry skies. And now you are the night light, the moon, thin crescent, waxing fuller, full moon, waning, thin crescent, new moon of no visible light.

Gently wax and wane back to your usual waking reality. Realize your own form, the fullness of your flesh, your own body and identity completely restored. Return slowly. Become wide awake and filled with energy. Open your eyes and stretch your body.

Your body is capable of performing unusual feats such as hand levitation. You move spontaneously into this state in emergencies. We have all heard stories about women who were able to lift cars off hurt children. Practicing hand levitation makes this ability conscious. To do hand levitation you relax and center yourself. As you become aware of the energy surrounding you, you move with that energy, letting that energy, not your will, lift your arm. Whenever you are in touch with the higher energy and can flow with it, your abilities and awareness increase.

After completing the exercise and before returning to your usual consciousness you may silently affirm to yourself, "I can use my hands or any part of my body to stop bleeding or pain when necessary." Once you have practiced several times you will be able to respond in an emergency. Of course, it will not be necessary to do the hand levitation first.

Hand Levitation

Sit in a relaxed position with your hands in your lap. Focus on your breathing, deepen and center yourself. You are very relaxed now and aware of the energy around you. You are surrounded by energy. You can let this energy carry your hand and arm off your lap and move your hand and arm higher and higher until it reaches your face.

Look at one of your hands. Look intently at that hand. Notice the energy around it. You may see it, feel it or sense it. Your hand is surrounded by energy. Let this energy lift your hand. Your hand and arm are slowly lifting up towards your face.

I am going to count from ten to one and by the time I reach the count of one your hand will touch your forehead. You will then take a deep breath and as you exhale your hand will return to your lap. Ten: the energy is surrounding and lifting your hand. Nine: your hand is growing lighter and lighter and moving higher and higher. Eight: the energy is carrying your hand right up to your face. Seven: your hand and arm are growing lighter and lighter and moving higher and higher. Six: your hand and arm, carried by the energy, are floating up to your face. Five: higher and higher, lighter and lighter. Four: the energy is moving your hand and it will soon reach your head. Three: higher and higher, lighter and lighter. Two: your hand is floating on the energy waves and it is moving towards your face. One: your hand and arm are feeling lighter and lighter and moving higher and higher. Let your hand touch your forehead.

Affirm to yourself, "I can use my hands or any part of my body to stop bleeding or pain. I will remember I have this ability and I will be able to use it when necessary." Now return easily to your usual awareness.

Whether or not your hand touched your forehead, you were still in the dimension where you could stop bleeding or pain. Sometimes people have to practice this exercise several times before their hand moves all the way to their face. People whose bodies are tight or tensed will need more practice.

AURAS

The electromagnetic field which surrounds all things is known as the aura. This force field may be seen psychically as a fluid, pulsating, oval-shaped ring of light, or it may appear as a swirling pattern of light with several colors shimmering through it. For some it will not translate into visual terms but will be sensed or felt. The aura has actually been photographed through the use of Kirlian photography, named after the Russian scientist who discovered the method.

A person who is highly skilled in aura reading may gather information about another's mental and emotional state, as well as information concerning her physical health and spiritual development, by observing the aura. Metaphysics teaches that the aura consists of seven interwoven rings of light, each revealing a different aspect of the person. The first ring reveals her state of health, the second her emotions, the third her intellectual make-up, the fourth her higher mind (imagination and intuition), the fifth her spirit, or the link between the individual and the cosmos, and the sixth and seventh reveal cosmic aspects. These last two are not usually visible on most people.

The aura is superimposed over the etheric, which is the invisible double of the physical body and is shed along with the physical at death. The etheric is the animal force of the body. It may be observed as a bluish haze around the body. Its thickness is determined by the health and vitality of the individual—one-half to four inches. The etheric body has the function of drawing in life energy from the atmosphere and distributing it along the system.

Once the physical body is shed at death, the etheric is shed also. However, it may take a while for the energy of the etheric to dissipate. It is something like turning the electric stove burner on so that it gets hot. When you turn it off, it will remain warm for a while. Often what people think of as a ghost is really the etheric energy of the person. It has no consciousness but follows the habits and patterns of the body to which it belonged. People who die suddenly, in an accident for example, may leave behind a strong etheric that will take some time to dissipate.

Most people can be taught to see auras; the first ring emanating from the physical etheric body is the one usually seen. It is not necessary to perceive the individual layers of the aura, or to distinguish the aura from the etheric, in order to gain information about the person you are observing. To perceive and diagnose the aura accurately, the person being observed must be naked: otherwise you are picking up vibrations from the clothing. For our purposes, however, the ability to distinguish a glow of light around the head and shoulders is sufficient.

When first observing auras, the colors are sometimes not perceived. Only a halo-shaped yellowish or whitish glow may be apparent or the colors, when observed, will be seen with the inner and not the physical eye, so that you may only feel or sense the color. With practice you will be able to perceive the colors visually. Although color is usually thought of as an absolute, it is really very subjective. Because of this variation and because the aura is continually pulsating, two people observing the same person may pick up different colors. Every emotion leaves its trace in the aura, so the colors fluctuate with your moods. Often, however, one or two colors will remain predominant. As you observe the aura for colors, allow the awareness of the color and its meaning to rise anew with each aura you observe. Here are some common color associations:

RED, energy, strength, courage
BRICK RED, anger
DEEP RED, sensuality
CRIMSON, loyalty
PINK, cheerfulness, optimism
ROSE, self-love
ORANGE, joy, vitality, balance of mental and physical
YELLOW, wisdom, creativity, spiritual
GREYISH YELLOW, fear
GREEN, ingenuity, compassion, growth
PALE GREEN, healing power
GREYISH GREEN, pessimism, envy
BLUE, spiritual, idealistic, imaginative, intellectual
GREYISH BLUE, melancholy
ICE BLUE, intellectual
PURPLE, spiritual power
ORCHID, idealism
WHITE, highly spiritual (rarely seen)
BLACK, depression, death (rarely seen)
BROWN, earthy
DULL BROWN, low energy
GREY, fear, boredom, repressed anger
GOLD, pure knowing and intuition
SILVER, similar to gold, very developed psychically

To observe the aura, you need to look with soft or blurred eyes. If you wear glasses, it is often easier to see the aura without them. Visualizing auras does not require the kind of intense focus needed for reading or driving. You need to relax and allow your self to perceive it. The aura surrounds the entire body, although it is more easily observable around the head and shoulders. It may take several attempts before you see the aura. You may see it at the first attempt but not trust it, feeling that it was only an after-image, or that your eyes were playing tricks on you.

Visualizing Auras. The person being observed should sit in front of a white or lightly colored background, as the aura is more easily perceived this way. It is also helpful if she closes her eyes and concentrates on sending energy into her head. This increases movement in the aura and makes it more readily visible. The person observing should close her eyes, relax and affirm to herself, "I can see my partner's aura." Then she can open her eyes and begin staring at the center of her partner's forehead. After a minute or so the aura will become visible. When first learning, keep your gaze on her forehead: if you look directly at the aura it will seem to disappear. If after a few minutes of concentrating it hasn't become visible to you, close your eyes and you may see the outline of her aura. Then open your eyes and continue observing.

Shaping Auras. The aura is continually vibrating and changing size, shape and color. To demonstrate changes in shape, have the person being observed concentrate on shaping her aura into a peak at the top of her head. To demonstrate changes in color, have the person observed concentrate fully on one specific color. If she is projecting strongly enough, you will be able to observe the color or shape she is sending. By observing the auras of several people you will see individual differences in sizes, shapes and colors.

Transferring Energy. To demonstrate how easily energy is transferred, have two people sit a slight distance apart. While you observe their auras, have them begin sending energy into each other's aura. In a few minutes you will see the auras vibrating, expanding and eventually meeting. It may appear as a flash of light between the two people. You may have to practice this several times. Success depends on your ability to relax and visualize the aura, as well as the ability of those you are observing to project their energy.

Sensing Auras. To sense auras, work with a partner. Relax and center yourself. Now slowly move your hands around your partner's body, about an inch or so away from it. Become aware of her energy. Notice how far away from her body you can perceive her energy. Notice if there are any places that feel cooler or warmer than others. Often in people who don't get much exercise the energy around their legs and feet will feel cooler or be harder to detect. Notice any other disruptions in the flow of energy. Places that feel very warm, the kind of heat associated with a sprained ankle, indicate blocked energy, as do unusually cool places. You will find that as you notice disruptions in the energy flow your partner will probably confirm them by saying something like, "Yes, I do have a backache," or "I did sprain my wrist some time ago."

Auric Protection. This exercise utilizes your body's natural defense mechanism, the aura. By visualizing your aura as a porous substance that allows energy to flow through it without getting caught, you'll be able to be in situations where the energy is negative and you won't be disturbed by it. Work with a partner who stands on the opposite side of the room facing you.

Relax and center yourself. Be sure that you are standing comfortably with your feet firmly on the floor, your weight distributed equally. You may want to focus on a spot an inch or so below your navel and imagine that you are inhaling through that spot. Now that you are grounded, begin to imagine that your body is a honeycomb, mesh screen, or any image that suggests you are open and porous. You are so porous that any energy coming towards you will flow right through you without affecting you in any way. Keep your attention completely focused on this image. Your partner will, without giving you warning, walk rapidly towards you, stopping only inches from your face. You will continue to hold your image so that you are not startled or affected by her energy. It will probably take several attempts before this happens. After you have practiced a while, switch roles with your partner.

Using images of honeycombs or screens will not only protect you from absorbing other people's energy, but also the energy from loud noises and any other bothersome thing in your environment.

Strengthening Auras. There are many breathing exercises and yoga postures that strengthen the aura. Some of the deep breathing exercises are described in Chapter One. Once you are comfortable with a deep breathing exercise in which you have increased the length of the inhalation and exhalation, you can add visualization to the practice. Establish a gentle rhythm of slow, deep breathing. Now imagine that you are suspended in the middle of a giant abalone seashell filled with light. The shimmering, irridescent pastel lights reflected from that seashell are swirling around you. As you inhale, fill yourself with that light. Feel it flowing throughout your body. You may also imagine that you are surrounded by beautiful music. Again, inhale this music.

CHAKRAS

The astral body, or energy body, is not separate from the physical body: it simply vibrates at a different frequency, making it invisible to normal eyesight. (See Chapter Four.) All of the energy bodies or levels of consciousness are intertwined and joined together at energy centers called *chakras*, the Sanskrit word for wheel, which may be seen psychically as swirling vortexes. Indian tradition often describes each *chakra* as a lotus, with each *chakra* or lotus having a different number of petals. This is a symbolic way of saying that each *chakra* vibrates at a different rate. We in the West looking at *chakras,* might use a different symbol.

Cosmic energy in the form of light rays is pulled into the body through the *chakras* and distributed along the spine so that it flows throughout the entire body. When the energy is absorbed into the body and is able to flow uninterrupted, the body is in balance and therefore healthy. If, for any reason, this harmonious flow is disturbed, difficulties arise.

Each *chakra* draws in a particular color ray. The red ray is drawn through the root or first *chakra* and supplies us with energy and vitality. The orange ray is drawn in through the second *chakra* and furnishes us with both physical and mental stimulation. The yellow ray is absorbed through the third *chakra* and aids in purification and stimulation of mental powers. The green ray is absorbed through the fourth *chakra* and is needed for balance and harmony. The blue ray is absorbed through the fifth *chakra* and its cooling properties help lower the body's temperature when necessary. The indigo ray is drawn in through the sixth *chakra* and is important for purification and proper functioning of the ears, eyes, nose and throat. The violet ray is drawn in through the seventh *chakra,* is soothing to the nervous system and aids in spiritual development.

Each *chakra* has different qualities ascribed to it. If there is a lack of, or a surplus of, a particular quality, an imbalance occurs and the flow of energy is disrupted. By focusing on the *chakras* you can become aware of the flow of energy throughout your being and notice any disruptions in that flow. You will pick up information concerning the reason for the disruption, if any, as well as possible solutions for re-establishing healthy energy patterns. This information comes to you through images, both symbolic and literal, colors, sensations and impressions. Observing these energy points enables you to uncover information about your physical, mental, emotional and spiritual state of being. You may learn to read your own or another person's *chakras.*

In reading *chakras,* as in any psychic work, there are many techniques that can be utilized. The number of *chakras,* their location and meanings, may differ according to the individual reader and the philosophical system the reading is based on.

I learned to read *chakras* from my dear friend, Seija Ling, who obtained the information psychically. She began utilizing it to help others through what she terms "seeings." Seija read my *chakras* and told me I could do this also. Shortly after that I tried it on another friend, and to my amazement I was able to see her energy and where it was blocked and explain why it was blocked and what she could do to unblock it.

41

I identify seven major *chakras* which correspond to points along the spine and head, and four secondary *chakras* which are located in the hands and feet. (Other systems of thought describe *chakras* differently.) The *chakras* are points in the astral body, but for convenience sake the corresponding location in the physical body is named. For those who are interested I have also included the Sanskrit names. The *chakras,* their locations and meanings as I know them, are as follows:

1. *(Mooladhara)* The base or root *chakra,* located at the base of the spine, has to do with your ability to survive, to make changes. People who can direct their energy are able to make changes necessary for their physical and emotional survival. The energy here corresponds to the earth element and is at the lowest level of vibration. It has to do both physically and emotionally with elimination. Just the right amount of energy here will give you a sense of stability; too much and you will become lethargic and afraid to make changes; not enough energy and you will feel unstable, not grounded, and you will perhaps fear for your survival.

2. *(Swadhishatana)* The second *chakra* is located between the ovaries for women and an inch or so below the navel for men. It has to do with reproduction and basic sexuality. It is referred to as the sacral, splenic or navel *chakra.* This *chakra* corresponds to the water element. The right amount of energy here allows you to remain flowing; not enough energy and you will literally dry up. This could cause sexual problems or diseases that have to do with hardening, like arthritis. If you have an excess of energy here, you may become too sensitive to other people. This *chakra* is concerned with the psychic ability of *clairsentience* (clear knowing). If the *chakra* is too open, you will absorb or become attached to other people's feelings continuously and become drained. It will be difficult for you to determine what is coming from you and what is coming from other people. It is better to learn to connect with people from the heart *chakra,* as it is less draining.

3. *(Manipura)* The third *chakra* is located in your solar plexus, which is about an inch or so above the navel. This *chakra* has to do with how you maintain yourself, how you create a balance within yourself. Corresponding to the fire element, it is an important center for healing, since it relates directly to the digestive system. With the right amount of energy here, you will absorb your food well, but if there isn't enough energy the food will be poorly absorbed.

4. *(Anahata)* The fourth, or heart, *chakra* is located between the shoulder blades. It is the center of compassion, understanding and love. Corresponding with the air element, it is a center for seeing clearly emotional connections with others. Not enough energy here and you become out of touch.

Too much energy here will make you overly sympathetic and anxious. You might manifest a saviour complex. When this *chakra* is balanced you can see clearly where your emotions are springing from.

5. *(Visudha)* The fifth, or throat, *chakra* is located at the base of the skull. It relates physically to the glands and emotionally to communication. Blocks in this *chakra*, difficulties with communication, can result in words literally being caught in your throat so that you become choked with emotion. This *chakra* corresponds to the element of space, or ether, and is the connecting bridge between the four lower *chakras* and the intuition and imagination of the brow *chakra*. The throat *chakra* is also known as the third ear, the space where you hear your inner or soul voice (the wise and knowing you). Vibrations of sound are very strong, so that chanting and singing help focus and balance the energies of the lower *chakras*. This is the center for developing the psychic ability *clairaudience* (clear hearing), the ability to hear voices. The voices are not to be confused with ego voices, voices of internalized parents or authority figures. You should not attempt to develop this ability unless you are a very stable, centered and emotionally sound person. Opening the throat *chakra* releases the creative energies, the creative word.

6. *(Ajna)* The sixth, or brow *chakra* is located between the eyebrows and known as the third eye. It is the space where conscious and unconscious knowledge join. In other words, this is the center where you connect with your Oversoul—the total you, that governing body that exists on the astral plane. Opening the third eye will give you the ability of *clairvoyance* (clear seeing), the psychic skill that allows you to see images, pictures, auras and *chakras*. *Ajna* means "command," and when you have fully developed your intuitive powers, you will truly be in command of yourself.

7. *(Sahasrara)* The seventh, or crown *chakra*, is located in the dome of the head. This is the spiritual center, the space of pure knowing and intuition. Opening this *chakra*, through meditation, makes possible the sense of peace that passes all human understanding. When this *chakra* is opened, the psychic abilities developed will far surpass those utilized in the third eye.

In addition to these *chakras* there are four secondary *chakras,* one in each hand and foot. The feet *chakras* have to do with the movement you make, the path you travel in life and your work. If these *chakras* are blocked, you may encounter difficulties in staying grounded. Interruptions in this energy could indicate an inability to take a stand or to stand on your own two feet. The hand *chakras* have to do with creativity and self-expression. Interruptions in the energy here could indicate problems with manipulation (either allowing yourself to be manipulated or acting in a manipulative way) and/or an inability to get a grasp on things.

Reading Your Own Chakras. To read your *chakras*, relax, deepen and protect yourself. When you are fully relaxed, bring your attention to the *chakras*, one at a time. Notice any colors, feelings, sensations or images. Work slowly and affirm that you will perceive and remember all that you experience. In the beginning you may want to look at only a few of the *chakras* and save the rest for another time. With practice you will be able to get a strong sense of your energy, if it is blocked, what is necessary to unblock it. When you are finished, return slowly to your usual awareness. This exercise is a more advanced exercise, and you may want to save it and try other exercises first.

Reading Other Peoples' Chakras. Once you are familiar with trance states and can easily relax and deepen, you may want to try reading a friend's *chakras*. The reading will be facilitated if you help your friend to relax and deepen also.

Sit comfortably and relax and deepen yourself. Then surround both your friend and yourself with a circle of protection. Affirm to yourself that you are clear and open to your friend and will uncover information that will be helpful and useful to her. When you are ready, focus on each *chakra* in turn, mentioning the *chakra*, its meaning and what you see and sense. When first learning, you may sense the energy patterns and colors without trying to interpret their meanings. Eventually the meaning will psychically become known to you also. You may see a symbol that doesn't make sense to you, but if you share it your friend may instantly connect with it. You may want to hold your hand over the area of the *chakra* you are reading to facilitate your receiving of impressions. When you are finished, fill yourself with white light and then return to your usual awareness. Then guide your friend to return also.

Once you are able to see or sense your *chakras*, you will want to clean them. This is a somewhat advanced healing technique that enables you psychically to remove anything that doesn't belong there. *Chakras* can become blocked by unexpressed emotions or by clinging to attitudes, feelings and beliefs that are no longer useful to you and therefore have become a drain on your energy. These attitudes and beliefs may be carry-overs from other dimensions or other lives, or they may be from your present life space.

Cleaning Chakras. To clean your *chakras*, relax, deepen and protect yourself. Now visualize your *chakras*, one at a time and notice what, if anything, is blocking them. It is not necessary to understand what is blocking the *chakras* in order to clean them. Remove the blockage by visualizing your hand reaching in and removing the stuff, or imagine the stuff draining away.

Another way to clean *chakras* is to begin at the heart *chakra* and pull all the stuff down through the lower *chakras* and imagine it draining off into the center of the earth. Then go back up into the throat *chakra* and pull all the stuff up through the upper *chakras* and out through the top of your head. Then see it dissipate harmlessly into the air.

Nature, it is said, abhors a vacuum. So don't leave your *chakras* empty as they may again collect undesirable stuff. Finish your cleaning by filling each *chakra* with a warm, golden light.

Cords. Everyone at one time or another allows other people to connect unconsciously with them. Whenever you absorb someone else's energy, you have established a connection. These connections may be perceived psychically as cords—long slender ropes extending from the *chakra* of the person who "corded" you to your *chakra,* or they may be sensed or felt.

It is not possible to be totally conscious at all times, so you won't always know when you are being corded. You may receive cords from strangers, as well as from those with whom you have ongoing relationships. However, on a very deep level, you cannot receive anything you don't agree to. No one can do anything to you without your permission. Often the permission is given at a deep unconscious level so that it may feel that you are getting something you didn't ask for.

The meaning of the cords depends on which *chakra* they are located in. Cords block your energy and should be periodically removed.

A cord in the feet *chakras* may indicate that a person is attempting to stop you from moving in the way that you wish. Perhaps this person is jealous of you.

Cords in the first *chakra* may indicate a person is depending on you for their survival. Unless this person is your child or someone you have agreed to take care of for a certain time, it is best to remove the cords.

Cords in the second *chakra* could indicate that someone is demanding emotional attention from you or that they are sexually attracted to you. Unless you desire that attention, it is best to remove the cords.

Cords in the third *chakra* may indicate someone wanting to use your energy instead of their own. This could cause a drain on you, even to the point of giving you a stomach-ache.

Cords in the fourth *chakra* mean that someone loves and cares for you. Cords here aren't as draining as in other places, but you may want to remove them so that your own energy is clear.

Cords located in the fifth *chakra* indicate that someone is trying to communicate with you. It is better to communicate directly, as cords here could cause a sore throat.

Cords in the sixth *chakra* indicate that someone is thinking strongly of you, perhaps wondering what you think of them. Cords here could cause headaches.

Cords located in the seventh *chakra* could mean that someone is trying to control you and you should remove them.

Removing Cords. To clear your energy and have it flowing smoothly and uninterruptedly, remove the cords. To do this, relax, deepen and protect yourself. Visualize the *chakras* one at a time and notice if there are any cords there. If there are and you wish to remove them, imagine that you are gently unplugging them. After you have removed all the cords, fill your *chakras* with light so they won't be left empty.

You may find it too exhausting to do all the *chakras* at one time, so clean half and leave the rest for later. The *chakras* may be left open, closed or varying degrees inbetween. This is done simply by visualizing them in the position you wish. After cleaning them, it is a good idea to close the lower three *chakras* (you will feel more grounded that way) and leave the upper ones open.

CHAPTER FOUR

Psychic Communication

You can communicate psychically with another human being by projecting your awareness into that being, communicating on a deep intuitive and nonverbal level. This kind of communication takes place more often than you realize. How many times when the phone has rung, have you known who it was before picking it up? How many times have you been thinking strongly of someone, only to run into them on the street in a place where you wouldn't ordinarily expect to meet them? Or received a letter from someone you'd been thinking of, yet hadn't heard from in years? Some people pass these occurrences off as mere coincidences, but the transfer of thoughts actually does occur.

Remember that everything in the universe is energy. So it is with thoughts. When you think, your brain sends out electrical impulses, and these impulses are capable of traveling through the air. We each have our own vibration, and it is possible for us to tune into each other's wave length just as on the radio we can tune in different stations. Naturally, we are protected from tuning in all the time. Imagine the chaos if you could hear everyone's thoughts when you were walking down a crowded street: this much stimulation could make you mentally unbalanced.

Whenever you become sensitive to another being and are able to pick up her vibrations, you are communicating on a psychic level. This happens when you're with a friend and you know what she's going to say before she says it. Or when you're able to know when someone close to you is extremely upset even though that person is far away. Psychic communication is possible with all living things—people, plants and animals. This diffused, female awareness is as important as the focused male awareness which is necessary to make our path in the outer world.

Conscious psychic communication occurs either when you project your astral body and visit another person or place, or focus on the person or

47

place and allow yourself to become open and receptive, thus becoming a channel for the information. You can thus gain information not always accessible through rational means. You should never descend to psychic snooping. We are morally obligated to be as clear as possible about our reasons for developing such abilities.

Projection is the ability you have of sending your thoughts or your awareness outside your physical body and into any person, object or point in the universe. Plant meditation, thought transference, psychic diagnosis, psychic readings and astral travel all involve this skill. Projection is also involved when you relive past experiences or move into other life spaces.

The exercise of plant meditation gives practice in communicating on a feeling and sensing level, thus bringing this kind of intuitive knowing to the conscious level. Tuning into a plant's vibration is a way of establishing a connection with the source of life itself, the universal harmony. Practicing this exercise also teaches you to focus and concentrate, a necessary step in meditation. With training you will create a quiet space where you will be open to hearing an inner voice. Plant meditation is also a beginning exercise in astral projection.

Plant Meditation

Sit in a circle around a healthy plant. Your eyes are closing and you are becoming more and more relaxed. Each part of your body is relaxing, a bit at a time, until you are fully relaxed. *Pause about two minutes.*

You are fully relaxed now. Create a circle of protection around yourself. You are relaxed and protected. Focus on your breathing and bring your breathing together. Inhaling, exhaling and pausing. *Pause about two minutes.*

And now slowly open your eyes and focus your awareness on the plant. You are very, very relaxed and all your attention is directed to the plant. Look only at the plant. Have a total awareness of the plant. *Pause about one minute.* Now I am going to take the plant away but you will continue to look at the place where the plant was and affirm a belief that the plant is still there. *Remove the plant and wait about one minute.*

Place the plant back into the center of the circle. Again focus your awareness on the plant, especially noticing if anything seems different for you.

Now, remain fully relaxed and relax even more. You are very fully relaxed. Slowly allow your consciousness to lift up, feel it lifting out and away from your physical body. Your awareness is moving away from your physical body and into the plant. You are moving into the plant. You may feel as though you are making believe, but this is the right feeling. Just move into the plant. Go into any part of the plant you like. Move into the leaves, the stems, the roots. Notice the light inside the plant. Notice the sound inside the plant. Notice the movement inside the plant. Notice the texture inside the plant. And now become the plant. Let your awareness join with the plant's awareness. Feel the movements in your body as you are the plant.

Now gently and easily move back into your own body. Let your awareness return to your physical body. Open your eyes and observe the plant again.

And seeing the plant again and knowing the plant has a consciousness, begin to communicate with the plant. Ask the plant if it has anything it can teach you. Close your eyes again and listen to the plant. What can it teach you? *Pause about one minute.*

The experience you have just had, of communicating with the plant and becoming the plant, is something that you often do on an unconscious level. You have learned to make the information conscious. This kind of knowing will enrich your experience and lead to greater understanding and compassion.

Return now to your usual awareness, your own identity fully restored.

THOUGHT TRANSFERENCE

Thought transference is the ability either to send your thoughts to another person or receive another person's thoughts into your body/mind. This often happens on an unconscious level. Realizing that the times you thought were coincidences are actually examples of thought transference will help to make this ability more conscious. Practice will increase this ability and enable you to focus and concentrate more intensely. Practice in receiving teaches you to become clear and sensitive.

To practice thought transference, decide ahead of time which kind of image you wish to send. For example, you may choose a Tarot card, a color, a number, an intense feeling, a single object or a simply worded message. It is not necessary to be in the same geographical location as your partner. The method is the same whether you are together or apart. Relax and deepen yourself. Your ability to send and receive images will be enhanced if you take the time to affirm to yourself that you are now in the space where you will find it very easy to send or receive messages telepathically. Then begin projecting. The person receiving should also deepen and clear her mind so she will be open to receiving. After a few minutes of intense concentration you can check and see if your message was received. Remember, if it wasn't, that doesn't disprove telepathy. It simply means you need more practice.

PSYCHIC READINGS

A psychic reading is another way of making contact with a person. You can learn about their physical and emotional state by receiving information through feelings, intuitions, sensations and images. The purpose of the reading is to obtain information that will be helpful and useful to the person being read. Keep in mind that you are trying to communicate this information in the best way possible for the person to understand and integrate it. You are being sensitive to the person's emotional condition at that time and are communicating the information in a way that will increase her self-awareness.

I have included three methods of psychic readings in which you are reading for a person who is present. Readings may also be done for people who are not physically present. However, you should not do a reading without the person's permission. Psychic readings may also be done for plants and animals.

In all readings, it is necessary for the psychic to relax, deepen and center herself. You must clear away all your thoughts and feelings for the moment so that you can become a clear channel for the information. The information will come to you in symbols or images, through feelings or bodily sensations, and/or by hearing voices.

We each have our own ways of receiving information, and we need to learn and trust them. There is no one correct way to do readings or any psychic work. What is important is the attitude and motives of the psychic. This kind of information is open to all of us. The strength and quality of the images, as well as the ability to interpret them, demand of the psychic that she work in all areas of her life to become a clear channel. This requires dedication, discipline and a sincere, loving heart.

Three Methods of Psychic Reading
1. Sit comfortably facing your partner. Both of you will relax, deepen and surround yourselves with a circle of protection.

The woman who is reading will extend her arms slightly with the palms facing up, and the woman being read will place her hands palms down but not touching the reader's hands. In this way you can feel the flow of energy. You may decide that you want to hold your partner's hands. Whatever is comfortable for you is the right way.

The reader then asks for guidance in receiving helpful information. To allow herself to remain open, the woman being read might imagine that she is swimming easily under water. This image makes her unconscious more easily accessible, but it is optional. The reader will open herself to her partner's vibrations and let images, feelings and sensations surface. As this happens she will share them with her partner. When the reader feels she has received all the information possible, both women will return to their usual awareness. The women may now exchange roles.

2. The two women sit facing each other with a candle between them. Using the candle as a focus, the women can relax, deepen and surround themselves with a circle of protection. The reader will ask for guidance in receiving helpful information. The woman being read will look at her partner and ask these questions several times. "Who am I? Who was I? Who will I be?" The reader will focus intently on her face, watching for changes and, as she observes them, she will share them. Then the women can return to their usual awareness and exchange roles.

3. The woman being read will sit in a chair and the reader will stand behind her with her palms either close to, or touching, her head. Both women will relax, deepen and protect themselves. The reader will ask for guidance in obtaining helpful information. She will then feel her partner's vibrations and share any information she receives. When she is finished, both women will return to their usual awareness and exchange roles.

Psychic Diagnosis. Psychic diagnosis is another method of doing a psychic reading. In this reading the women will read for people not present, rather than reading for each other. A diagnosis may be done on a person, plant or animal. To use this method, work with a partner. One woman will act as a guide and the other as the psychic. It is not necessary for the psychic to know the person she is reading or to be in the same geographical location with her.

The guide's role is to help the psychic relax, deepen and become centered in the dimension where she will be able to receive information. A guide needs to be sensitive to the psychic and encourage her to keep talking as she diagnoses. In presenting the case the guide will give the psychic the name, age and address of the person.

When learning diagnosis it's a good idea to pick a person, plant or animal that has some injury or illness which you have knowledge of. This way you can verify the diagnosis. Pick only living persons, and not ones who are seriously ill, because the sensations picked up from the latter may be too intense for a beginning psychic.

If the psychic is picking up vibrations so strongly that she is uncomfortable, you can lessen her involvement by saying, "I'm going to count from one to five and by the time I reach the count of five you will be receiving information at a level that is comfortable for you. *Count.* Your involvement has decreased and you are receiving information at a comfortable level."

If the psychic would like to increase contact (and this is more often the case) you can say, "I'm going to count from one to five and by the time I reach the count of five you will be in close, comfortable contact with 'Jane.' " *Count.* "Your involvement with Jane has increased and you are receiving more information."

If everything is completely off, and this is rare, the psychic could have picked up the wrong person. Tell her you think a different person is coming through and ask her if she is aware of someone else. If this doesn't work, have her send healing to the person and then remove the image.

If the guide becomes too specific in her feedback, it could degenerate into questions and answers rather than a steady flow of impressions. Save feedback until after the psychic returns to her usual awareness. You may say, however, "Yes, Jane does have trouble with her stomach," after the psychic has completed the information and before she has returned to her usual awareness. This will give her an idea of how she feels when the information is correct. Suggestions are more easily absorbed while in the trance state, so remember to talk in a positive way when someone is in that dimension. For example, it is better to say, "I'm not aware of that information," rather than "That's not correct."

If the psychic isn't pouring out a steady stream of information, here are some suggestions. Don't use them all in one session. The guide talks only enough to encourage the psychic to respond.

1. Imagine that you are Jane and perceive the world as she perceives it.
2. Follow Jane through the day and notice her actions, feelings and reactions.
3. Watch Jane carefully as she goes through some specific movement such as eating or running.
4. Run your physical hands over a specific body part.

5. If the psychic is making any physical movement, ask what she is experiencing.

To assist you in your practice, I have included a sample of what a guide might do and say in leading the psychic in her diagnosis.

Psychic Diagnosis

Lie down comfortably and relax now. Let your whole body fully relax, beginning with your toes and extending the deep relaxation throughout your entire body until it reaches your head and you are very fully relaxed.

Use a calming, deepening image and let me know when you are ready to continue.

As you continue to move deeper, deeper and deeper, know that you have the ability to send your awareness into another person. And by sending your awareness into this person you will be able to receive information about this person, knowledge about her physical and emotional being that will be helpful to her. Continue moving deeper, deeper and deeper into the realm of intuitive awareness.

Let me know when you are as deep as you wish to go. *Wait for her to signal you.*

And now I'm going to give you the name of the person you will contact. You will come into very close, comfortable contact with this person.

Let the image of (Jane Smith, 25 years old from Boston, Massachusetts) come into your awareness. The image of Jane Smith has appeared. Explain to her that you are learning psychic diagnosis and would like to use her being to learn from. If she says "yes," we'll continue; if not we'll pick another person. (If "yes," continue. If "no," have her erase the image and give her another name.) Now surround Jane and yourself with a circle of protection. Affirm to yourself that both you and she are protected from all harm.

And now see vividly before you or have a vivid awareness of Jane. Let your consciousness move into hers. Feel what she feels, experience what she experiences. As you have a full awareness of Jane, notice any feelings, sensations or images you are receiving from her and let me know. You may feel as though you are imagining this but that is the right feeling. Remember this is a practice session. Continue to have a full awareness of Jane and as your images and feelings arise, share them with me. *Listen about ten minutes.*

Remain focused on Jane and tell me if there is anything you may have forgotten to mention. *Pause about one minute.* Now send healing energy to Jane and let me know when you are finished. Thank Jane and remove her image from your awareness. Let her awareness fade from yours. Let go of any feelings, sensations or images that you may have picked up from her. Let Jane leave your awareness completely and know that your own identity is completely restored.

Move gently and easily up to your usual waking reality, feeling wide awake and filled with energy.

ASTRAL PROJECTION

The astral body, the less dense version of the physical body that encases it, can be projected at will. The astral, also known as the energy body or body of light, leaves the physical body each night during sleep. It is connected to the physical body by what is called the silver cord, until death when the cord is severed. Many times when you awaken with a jolt, the jolt is caused by the astral body rapidly re-entering the physical body. These nightly trips are natural occurrences. Most of us don't remember them, however, or it we do, they are confused with dreaming. How often have you awakened from a dream so vivid that you couldn't tell whether it was a dream or a real event? Often the very vivid specific dreams are actually very real astral travel.

You can learn to remember your nightly astral travels by telling yourself you will. Each night before going to sleep, relax yourself and say three times, "I will sleep comfortably and remember where I travel in my astral." It may take a week or so of doing this but eventually you will remember.

With practice you can learn to project your astral body whenever you wish. As long as you do this as a way of gaining knowledge and not as a way of snooping, you have nothing to fear. If the idea of astral travel is very frightening to you, then it's best not to attempt it. Researchers have found that attempting to project astrally alters the respiration. This could create difficulty for people with heart trouble. So if you have any such difficulty, don't attempt astral projection.

Projection, done with the right attitude, can be fun and an interesting way to travel. You can gain experience not ordinarily accessible to you, such as visiting faraway places. Astral travel demands a disciplined mind. Once you have left the physical body you are no longer limited in the way the physical body is. For example, you can travel through walls and other seemingly solid objects. You respond instantly to thought; whatever you think will happen.

Unless your friends like having you drop in unexpectedly, don't travel to their homes uninvited, even in your astral body. Let them know you are practicing this kind of traveling. To prove to yourself that you have indeed traveled to where you thought you traveled, try going to a friend's house that you have not yet visited in your physical body. While there, notice at least two specific details; you can check them out at a later time. If you are the type of person who doesn't remember lots of physical details but picks up the tone of the place you are visiting, this will also be true when you are astral traveling. If you're visiting a friend to see how she is doing, you'll probably notice her feelings more than her furniture. After all, that's what you're there for. Just try to get yourself to notice one or two concrete things to help you verify your visit.

I have included one exercise to guide you in your attempts to project. You may also practice alone. Remember to choose a time when you will be uninterrupted for at least thirty minutes. Allow yourself to relax completely, then use the circle of protection and begin to imagine that your astral body is lifting out and away from your physical body. You might want to imagine your astral body leaving a bit at a time: let your legs and feet lift out and so on until your entire body is out. You might want to imagine that you are traveling in the same way you would in your physical body: leave your apartment, get in your car, etc. The important thing to understand is that this is a natural way to travel—you do it each night while sleeping—so let yourself relax and then travel. People have reported different sensations when leaving the physical, most of them pleasant floating effects. However, sometimes it can be jolting to leave or return, and it takes practice to accomplish this with ease.

Astral Projection

Relax, deepen and protect yourself. You are very relaxed now, so very, very relaxed. Every muscle and tendon is loose, limp and relaxed. You are completely surrounded by a moving, shimmering circle of light. Feel this beautiful circle of light. Let this light enter your body now. Let this liquid light pour into your body. Let your body become filled with this light. And now you have become a body of light.

Let this body of light lift out and away from your physical body. Just leave your physical body there on the floor. Your consciousness is with your light body that is traveling out and away from your physical body. And know that your physical body will remain in this room and it will continue to breathe and to function, but your consciousness is contained in this body of light that is being lifted out and away from your physical body. And know that your body of light will return to your physical body. But for now you will learn to travel between dimensions, to travel very, very far or travel only a short space away, if that is what you wish to do. And you may travel now, protected by that light, and in fact you are that light. Your physical body will remain safely in this room.

And now you are traveling in your light body. Travel around this room. Fly up to the ceiling in your light body and then travel all around the room, flying all around the room, exploring the high corners of this room.

And now fly over your physical body and see your physical body lying there. And now find to your amazement that you are traveling straight up, traveling right through the ceiling and right through the roof. And it is very easy for you to do this. And now you are floating high above the house. Moving higher and higher and now let yourself fly high above the earth. Fly high above the earth but not so high that you lose my voice. Hear my voice and let it carry you higher and higher.

And now safely guided by my voice begin to fly lower and lower, flying or simply floating down. Moving back and down to earth. Down and down through the roof, back into this building, back into this room and continue flying lower and lower. Flying down past your body. Down beneath your physical body, down and down. Moving on down into the center of the earth. Moving on down and down and still hearing my voice as you move on down.

And now feel your consciousness in that light body and let it travel up. Let it float up and up, moving through the earth, moving up and back through the earth's crust and moving up and back to your physical body, yet not entering it because you are now moving to the side. Moving to the left side, moving out and away, moving up and left or down and left, however you want to move, but moving to the left, very far out to the left side. Traveling faster and faster or slower and slower, because speed is relative. But you are traveling in that light body, traveling very far away yet still guided by my voice.

And now coming back again, moving back along until you come to your body again and seeing your body but not entering it because you are now moving to the right, moving up and right or down and right, moving out to the right. Moving faster and faster or slower and slower because speed is relative, but moving to the right, safely guided by my voice and moving to the right.

And now moving back again, moving back towards your body and you are hovering over your body but not entering it yet because you have one more direction to travel. You will now travel very quickly to your home, to the place where you live and visit there for a while. You are now at your home. *Pause about one minute.*

And now leaving your home and returning to your physical body. Your body of light is now hovering over your physical body and you can see your physical body very clearly and you know that it was well taken care of while you were traveling in your light body. And now you may slowly and gently enter your physical body again. Just ease your light body back into your physical body very gently now. You are now back in your physical body. Become aware of the fullness of your physical body once again. And know that you have a body of light and that body of light is encapsulated in your physical body. And know that your body of light may travel without your physical body if that is your wish.

And now hear my voice calling you back, back into your physical body, back into this room, back to your usual waking reality. And you are wide awake and filled with energy. Whenever you are ready open your eyes and stretch your body.

CHAPTER FIVE

Healing

Women have always been healers. They were the unlicensed doctors and anatomists of western history. They were the abortionists, nurses, and counsellors. They were the pharmacists, cultivating healing herbs and exchanging the secrets of their uses. They were midwives, travelling from home to home and village to village. For centuries women were doctors without degrees, barred from books and lectures, learning from each other, and passing on experiences from neighbor to neighbor and mother to daughter. They were called "wise women" by the people, witches and charlatans by the authorities. Medicine is a part of our heritage as women, our history, our birthright.*

The ancient art of healing is rooted deeply within woman-caring and woman-sharing. From the very beginnings of time, women have been most intimately connected with birthing, nurturing, preparing and storing food, and caring for the sick and dying. These experiences have led us to become both sensitive and compassionate—and through them we became the inventors of the first healing potions and medicines.

Before the advent of modern technology people lived closer to the earth. The rhythm of their lives flowed with the rhythm of the seasons. People were guided by intuition: the connections between inner and outer worlds, body and mind, thought and action, were strongly sensed and felt. Healing is based on these connections. It is an art that takes as its premise the existence of a common life force in the universe which connects all living things. It is this force, this life energy, that is channeled between people when healing is given.

When our bodies, minds and spirits are connected, we flow in harmony with the universe and have an abundance of energy. We are well and whole. The life force flows from the universe into and out of our bodies in a continuous cycle. If we are tense and block the energy, we become tired or sick. Healing is effected when the blocked energy is released. Getting plenty of exercise, fresh air, sunshine and adequate rest; eating a healthy diet and hav-

---

*Barbara Ehrenreich and Deirdre English, *Witches, Midwives and Nurses: A History of Women Healers* (New York: The Feminist Press, 1973), p. 1.

ing the ability to express emotions freely; and maintaining a positive attitude —all enable the life energy to flow freely. Psychic healing uses breath energy and visual images to maintain this free flow of energy.

There is no secret to healing. It is an ability we all possess. Life energy is always around us and always available for our use, as long as we are open to receiving it. Healing energy can be experienced as light, color or sound vibrations and/or as any visual image that suggests healing to us.

The healer sees herself as a channel through which the healing energy flows. She draws this energy into her body either by an effort of will or simply by allowing herself to be receptive to it. She may use it to heal herself and/or she may channel it into other living things. Healing is an act of loving; loving is an act of healing. The healer is also healed each time she uses her body as a channel for healing energy. She is never drained; she never sends her own energy.

The healing process is not completed simply by becoming receptive to the universal energy. It involves more than using visual images, laying on of hands or breath energy. Healing is a journey deep within oneself—a search for soul, the essence of the self. It seeks to balance the inner and outer worlds, to connect and to integrate. Healing is the reuniting of the body, mind and spirit.

This inner journey is a gradual process of developing greater self-awareness. Confronting our beliefs about sickness and health is a necessary part of it. We

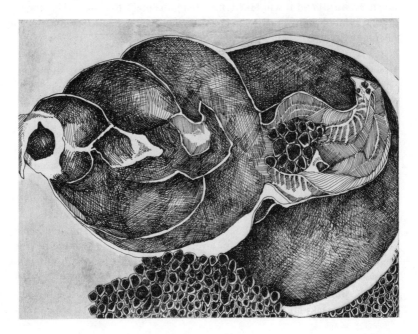

have all learned to be sick. We have assumed that our bodies are weak and break down easily, that only trained professionals can heal. We have learned to cope with unpleasant situations by becoming ill rather than by confronting situations directly and honestly.

Sickness is your body's way of telling you that something isn't quite right. As you learn to respond to these messages early on (at the first stiffening of your muscles, for example) you can change your course of action and eliminate much illness. Notice when you get sick. What was happening to you just prior to the illness? Are you able to slow down and relax, or is getting the flu the only thing that stops you? How often have you been angry or sad and not expressed it only to find that your back is aching? Is getting sick the only way you know how to ask for love and attention?

Diseases are really metaphors which you should look at closely. Where are the places in your body that you hold tension (legs, shoulders, neck)? Which parts of your body break down most frequently? What do these body parts represent to you: everyone has her own private associations for various body parts and diseases which can help in understanding why the disease occurred.

Healing is a process of discovering where your energy is blocked and learning ways of unblocking it. Though healing can be instantaneous, more often it is a gradual process of becoming more self-aware. Your body didn't break down overnight and it will take longer than one night to heal it. Understanding the symbolism of the disease enables you to understand why the blockage of energy occurred; this understanding aids the release.

An illness often provides you with an opportunity for self-discovery and growth. When they are healthy, most people don't take the time to reflect on themselves—who they are, where they came from and where they are going. It may be only during times of illness or crisis that they are forced to take a good look at themselves. If you make use of such times to become more self-aware, you are on your way to leading a healthier, happier and more fulfilling life. (It is not always possible to examine your beliefs and feelings during the height of an illness. At that time you may need to use all your energy to ease your suffering. Later, you will be better able to assess what brought the situation about.)

We all have a life-death struggle within us. When a person contracts a serious disease, she has identified with death and a choice is demanded between life and death. This calls for a very serious appraisal of oneself. Who am I and where am I going? How and why did I get involved in the situation I now find myself in? What needs to be done in order to get out of this situation? Am I willing to do it? When such a problem is encountered, a person needs to seek out the help of healers, therapists, chiropractors and doctors, and to decide which treatments will be most beneficial to her. These treatments, of course, are not necessarily mutually exclusive.

I have included a list of illnesses and body parts and their common associations. This list is in no way intended to replace healing treatments. It is put forth as a beginning to help you come to a place of inner clarity. There are no absolutes. The reason your friend broke her leg may not be the reason you broke yours. Understanding the why of your illness and taking more responsibility for your health does not mean you should put yourself down when you get sick. This kind of negative self-judgment will only hinder your progress. Nor is it for you to decide why someone else is sick. You cannot judge the state of a person's evolution or spiritual development by the state of their health. Suffering doesn't necessarily make you more evolved. Believing that it does may limit your development. Physical health doesn't necessarily make you more evolved either. Each situation is unique. Making the connections between emotions and disease doesn't always liberate you from sickness. Every situation can be improved, however, and usually improved much more than you are aware of.

Sometimes you may have an illness that you can see no reason for, at least not in your present life. This could mean that it is a bleed-through from another life space. Some people refer to this as a karmic illness. Yet, this also may be changed. Often a child born with a disability has chosen to learn something through the situation that disability presents. (This does not mean you don't attempt to eliminate the child's suffering. That would be a gross misinterpretation of karma.) Or you may have chosen on a very deep level to have a specific illness in order to learn more about that illness or to learn a lesson that you felt could best be learned through suffering the illness. Sometimes a short period of trauma is necessary to change the body's vibration. Whatever the reason for your illness, you can be sure that by sincerely striving to understand it you are growing and changing.

The following is a list of ailments and body parts and their common associations:

Headaches: feelings of inadequacy; pressure to conform or be perfect; too heady, not connected with feelings or body.

Eye problems: situation that you don't want to see.

Ear problems: something that you don't want to hear.

Teeth problems: difficulty expressing anger and aggression.

Gum and mouth problems: difficulties with speaking out; inability to express anger; difficulty in feeding (nurturing) oneself.

Sore throat: inability to say what's bothering you—words are caught in your throat; problems with communication; feeling choked with emotion.

Arm and hand problems: inability to get a grasp on things; problems with manipulation; inability to express yourself creatively.

Heart problems: inability to express feelings of love and attachment; deep sadness; literally having a broken heart.

Asthma or breathing problems: person, attitude or situation that is suffocating you; something you can't get off your chest.

Stomach or digestive disturbances: person, attitude or situation you can't stomach; something you can't digest; inability to absorb or inability to eliminate.

Vomiting: trying to release painful or negative feeling.

Ulcers: attitudes or situation literally eating away, deep-seated anger.

Skin problems: anger or irritations not as deep as ulcers because skin is really on the surface.

Diarrhea: too hyper; not absorbing something necessary or trying to eliminate negative feeling about self.

Constipation: refusal to let go of situation, person or attitude; clinging to emotions or beliefs.

Leg and foot problems: difficulty with dependence; inability to stand on your own two feet; inability to acknowledge the interdependence of all living things.

Knee problems: inflexible attitude; being weak-kneed; lacking humility; feeling as though you have gotten yourself in too deep.

Varicose veins: anger, feeling the urge to kick someone so the blood rushes into the legs and becomes blocked.

Colds, running nose: inability to cry.

Flu: may be one of the little suicides because of the sudden onset, body is completely exhausted and depression follows. (Smoking or any habit that is harmful to your health may be termed a "little suicide.")

Vaginitis or problems with reproductive organs: negative sexual feelings or attitudes; inability to let go of painful sexual experiences; problems related to nurturing or being nurtured.

Arthritis: problem releasing and expressing anger, joints clench and wear down.

Shoulder problems: feeling like you carry the weight of the world on your shoulders; saviour complex.

Backache: carrying too much responsibility; trying to be Superwoman; struggling with dependency, having no backbone; rigid or inflexible attitude; misuse of will power.

Cancer: A tumor is a growth that engulfs and devours. The cells are multiplying not in an effort to sustain life but in a way that destroys life. Beginning tumor cells look very similar to beginning fetal cells, but the end result is death rather than birth.

In a culture such as ours where the female energies, the yin, or the mother is repressed, growth is thwarted. People struggle to grow psychically, spiritually, emotionally and when this growth is blocked cancer may be the result. All individuals need to develop the nurturing or mothering aspect of themselves. When this is denied in both women and men, they can over-mother by giving too much to others and nothing to self or develop a clinging attitude, an inability to let go of feelings, attitudes or people. An imbalance can also be caused by not being able to "mother," an inability to nurture self or others.

SELF-HEALING

To practice self-healing relax, deepen and protect yourself. If you wish you may create a special mind space just for healing. Go to that space and visualize yourself surrounded by healing energy. This energy may be visualized as light, color or sound vibrations, or as any image that suggests healing to you. It may also be sensed or felt as a warm glow or tingling sensation.

Self-healing may be practiced at any time that is convenient for you. If you wish to practice before going to sleep, you can suggest that the healing will continue throughout the night and you will awaken relaxed, alert and refreshed. Before going to sleep is also an excellent time for repeating healing affirmations. Relax yourself—a good idea each night because it ensures a restful sleep. Often people fall asleep just as tense as when they are awake, so sleeping really doesn't refresh and heal them. Once you are relaxed, repeat affirmations like these: "Perfect health is the natural state of my being." "I will have a comfortable, restful sleep and awaken filled with energy." "Each cell of my body is regenerating, my heart is pumping steadily and strongly, my lungs are filling with healing energy, and as I exhale I am releasing all toxins." "My spine is straight, my muscles and tendons are relaxed." "I am a strong, vibrant and energetic woman."

Healing Space is an exercise in self-healing.

Healing Space

Relax, deepen and protect yourself. Visualize yourself on a deserted beach. Wander along the winding seashore, conscious of the warmth of the sun on your body and the salty sea air. Listen to the sound of the waves washing against the shore and be comforted by it. Continue walking now, finding yourself moving among the sand dunes. And here you come upon the entrance to a cave. Enter that cave now, guided by my voice and move through the labyrinth of time. Go down passages winding down and into the earth. Moving on now to your left you come to the healing space. It is a very beautiful and serene space where you are in touch with the calm, expansive power within you and you are receiving pure energy from the universe.

See and sense this vibrant, pulsing energy all around you. You are bathed in the warmth and glow of this energy. Draw it into your body as you inhale. Use this energy as a gentle massage to break up tension and as you exhale let the tension drain away. Feel the energy circulating throughout your body just as your circulation does. Let the energy fill every cell and tissue. Let it sink deep into the marrow of your bones.

Breathe deeply, inhaling this healing energy. Direct this energy into your legs and feet. Let it flow into your legs and feet just as your circulation does. As you exhale let the tension drain away. Healing energy is flowing into your legs and feet and your body is returning to its natural state of health.

Breathe deeply and send the healing energy into your pelvic area. Let the energy move through your pelvis, breaking up any tension. And as you exhale let the tension drain away.

Breathe deeply and send the energy into your abdomen now. Let the energy fill all your organs. Every cell and tissue is filled with healing energy. Healing is simply a matter of re-establishing healthy energy patterns as you are doing now.

Breathe deeply and fill your chest with healing energy. Let every cell and tissue fill with healing energy. As you exhale you are releasing tensions and toxins and your body is returning to its natural state of health.

Breathe deeply and send the healing energy into your back. Your back, shoulders and neck are filled with healing energy. All your muscles and tendons are fully relaxed. Healing energy is flowing through your back, shoulders and neck and you are returning to a perfect state of health.

Breathe deeply and send the healing energy into your arms and hands. Let the energy flow down your arms just like your circulation does.

And breathe deeply again, inhaling the healing energy. Send it into your head now. Fill your lips, your jaw, your cheeks, your eyes, nose, mouth and ears. Feel the energy flowing into your scalp. This energy is always around you and always available for your use.

Relax in this healing space a while. Fill yourself with the Goddess essence. Feel and sense your connections with the whole of the cosmos. This is your space, you have created it. You may return here whenever you feel the need to relax and open yourself to the healing energy of the universe. Whenever you are ready you may leave the cave and walk back along the ocean, walk up and back to your usual waking reality. You will return relaxed, refreshed and filled with healing energy.

HEALING COMMON AILMENTS

There are specific breathing exercises that will heal and relieve symptoms of sore throats and colds. Try this breathing exercise when you feel a sore throat coming on. Curl your tongue like a cat does and then begin inhaling through your mouth and exhaling through your nose. Your mouth will feel very dry, but try to keep this up for several minutes. Repeat it every hour until the soreness is gone. I've tried this and it works.

For stuffy noses this exercise is great. Place your thumb and index finger on either side of your nose right under your eyes. Use your left hand if you are right-handed, and vice versa. Now use pause breathing. Inhale through your nose, exhale through your nose, and while the air is out of your lungs imagine healing energy filling your nose, breaking up the congestion. When you must breathe again do so, and continue the exercise. Try to do it for at least two minutes at a time, keeping your lungs empty for as long as you can while visualizing the healing energy. You should hear a little crackle as the congestion breaks up. Do this exercise as often as necessary until you are healed.

This exercise may also be used for breathing problems associated with asthma. This time place the thumb and index finger of your left hand if you are right-handed, and vice versa, on either side of your throat, right over your collar bone. Use the same breathing technique. You may also do this placing your fingers lower on your chest. Try both finger locations and see which is more helpful for you. The breathing is the same.

ELIMINATING PAIN

Pain is always a signal that something is wrong. Make sure you know the cause of the pain before you work to remove it. For example, what seems like a simple stomach-ache could be appendicitis. If you remove pain from something like a sprained ankle, remember that even though you no longer feel the pain the ankle may still be bruised and need more time to heal fully—so don't be too quick to walk on it again.

You can stop pain by deepening yourself and then telling yourself that you will count from ten to one and by the time you reach the count of one you will feel clear and comfortable. Then count slowly and when you reach the count of one you will be clear and comfortable. If the pain is severe you may have to do this several times and/or have a friend deepen you and give the suggestions. Always phrase the affirmations in a positive way. If, for example, you have a headache say, "My head feels clear and comfortable" rather than "My headache is gone." Use the present tense when repeating the affirmation saying, "My head feels" rather than "My head is going to feel." Otherwise your mind will not connect with the words.

COLOR HEALING

In healing by color, the healer visualizes the needed color and then breathes it into her body or channels the color into the body of the person she is healing. You may use color healing with laying on of hands—sending the needed color through your hands and into the body of the person you are healing. Or you may send the needed color to the person without touching them or without them being in the same room.

To pick the necessary color, deepen and ask yourself what color or colors this person needs. Here is a list of common color associations:

Red: strength, energy and vitality; increases circulation and reduces pain.

Orange: uplifting for the nervous system; used for chest troubles and bronchitis.

Yellow: a nerve builder; reduces swelling and increases the flow of bile; used for skin troubles.

Golden Yellow: a lubricant; eliminates constipation.

Green: increases vitality; dissolves blood clots; restores balance.

Yellow Green: use for the loss of enthusiasm and regeneration of body.

Blue Green: calming and reduces fevers.

Turquoise: tranquilizes and relieves headaches.

Blue: anesthetizes and reduces fevers; lowers blood pressure.

Violet: soothes, relieves cramps and induces sleep; relieves psychological distress.

Magenta: good for heart problems and emotional equilibrium.

Indigo: purifies; relieves swelling; ear and eye problems; sedative.

Purple: stimulates veins; relieves indigestion.

White: it's nice to end with this inspirational color.

SENSING HEALING ENERGY

Sit in a comfortable position. Place your feet firmly on the ground and/or use a mental image to ground yourself. Now relax, deepen and protect yourself. Visualize yourself surrounded by healing energy. Rub your hands together quickly to get the energy flowing. As you inhale draw in the healing energy, and as you exhale release any tension. After a few minutes of this, continue to inhale the healing energy but as you exhale send it down your arms and out your hands or fingertips. Hold your hands palms together but not touching. Notice the sensations between your hands. Play around with this energy for a few minutes. Move your hands closer together and then farther apart. Can you feel the energy? Can you notice any differences in distance? Once you have a sense of this energy and your ability to project it out your hands, you are ready to send it to another person. Return to your usual awareness.

HEALING FOR OTHERS

Healing should be sent only to those who request it. Everyone has the right to privacy, the right to their own illnesses, and unless healing is requested you are invading their space. Giving someone space does not mean you ignore their pain. You make it known by your actions and your words that you are ready to help if and when they desire it. You can only do for someone what they will allow you to do—frustrating as this may be for you. When giving healing you are helping the person to heal herself. You are aligning yourself with the person and with the universal energy. You are channeling this energy, not your own, into the person.

Laying on of Hands

Sit with your feet on the ground and/or use a mental image to ground yourself. Relax, deepen and protect yourself. Rub your hands together quickly to get the energy flowing.

Place your hands on the woman who is being healed, one hand on her forehead and one hand on her belly. If there are more healers, place hands wherever you feel comfortable.

Breathe slowly and inhale the healing energy. As you exhale send it down your arms, out through your hands and into the woman you are healing. Visualize her as well and healthy. Continue to send the healing energy for five or ten minutes (longer if you wish), and then slowly remove your hands.

Absent Healing

Sit with your feet on the ground, and/or use a mental image to ground yourself. Relax, deepen and protect yourself. Visualize the person you are healing as well and healthy. Visualize the energy radiating from your solar plexus and moving outward and into the body of the person you are healing. Continue sending healing energy as long as you wish and then return to your usual awareness.

CHAPTER SIX

Creating
Our Own Reality

We create our own reality. The experiences we have and the situations we find ourselves in are the result of our inner reality—the feelings, thoughts and beliefs we hold. No one is simply an unfortunate victim of circumstances. We are the creators of our lives.

As women we've been taught to see ourselves as helpless and powerless victims, unable to act because of the forces that surround us. It isn't an easy task to realize that we have a part in creating these circumstances. This task is made all the more difficult by our feelings of guilt and our belief that punishment is justified. To take responsibility for creating an unpleasant situation means that we understand and accept our part in its creation. Accepting responsibility is a positive action involving owning some action, attitude or belief. It is the acknowledgment that you have either consciously or unconsciously participated in the creation of a situation. It does *not* imply blame. Blame is a negative action involving condemnation. Accepting responsibility for your own life doesn't imply guilt, blame or the idea that we should not be working with others whose life circumstances are more unfortunate than our own.

We create our own reality. Accepting this means having an awareness that we are more than just our physical bodies; it means acknowledging that the world consists of far more than what can be perceived by the five senses; it means understanding that change starts from within and that our mind is the cause and our experiences are the result. It is knowing that our feelings/thoughts are energy forms which may be manifested on a physical level.

Most of us have experiences with the world beyond the physical. We get glimpses of it through our dreams and intuitions, when we respond to someone's vibrations or the energy they are sending, when we see images and auras, or when we listen to that inner voice. We've been taught to deny the existence of many of these occurrences. Fortunately, awareness and acceptance of the non-physical world is changing. The feminist movement encourages us to take ourselves seriously, to see that our dreams, intuitions, hunches and feelings are important and valid. Scientists are now able to photograph the human aura, and bio-feedback machines have empirically demonstrated that we can lower our heartbeat and metabolic rate through meditation. Physicists are discovering things about energy that metaphysicians have been saying for centuries. Psychologists affirm the importance of our dreams and their messages to us.

Each time we send out a feeling/thought, energy is released. This happens whether or not we are conscious of it happening, and whether or not the thought is negative ("I'm stupid") or positive ("I can do this"). Energy itself is a neutral force: its use determines whether it will assume a positive or negative form. If the feelings/thoughts we project are positive, the energy that is built will eventually manifest in positive situations. If feelings/thoughts are negative, the energy that collects will assume a negative form.

Thoughts are things, energy vibrations, like everything else in the universe. To create something, we can think it into existence. This doesn't mean, of course, that if you become angry and wish someone dead, they will immediately die. Nor does it mean that you can close your eyes and summon a new car to appear in your driveway. And it certainly doesn't mean that you don't have to do anything except sit around thinking, dreaming and wishing. What it *does* mean is this: everything created in this universe was once a thought. As you begin to become aware of the power of thoughts, you can use them creatively to make positive changes in your life. Feelings, thoughts and beliefs are not permanent: they are always changing, or capable of being changed.

To use your thoughts to create more positive situations for yourself, you must first learn to control them. This isn't the same as repressing them. Controlling your thoughts means that you have only those thoughts and images in your mind that you wish to create and, secondly, that you are able to stop the flow of images, to still the mind, at will.

How can this be accomplished? Begin by listening to yourself and noticing the feelings you have, the attitudes and beliefs you express and the pictures you form in your mind. Do they limit you? For instance, do you feel that your experiences are worse than anyone else's? Do you think that you don't have the money or the talent to do what you want? These thoughts will limit your possibilities. In the beginning it is necessary just to notice the thoughts without attempting to change them. Awareness is the first step. Don't criticize or condemn yourself for these feelings. Don't pretend they don't exist. After you have observed your thoughts, feelings and beliefs for a while you can decide if they're the kinds of things you wish to express. If so, fine. If not, you can begin to change them. Filling your mind with positive images can happen only when the negative ones are released, not repressed. Use the exercises in Chapter Two to let go of attitudes, feelings and thoughts that you consider either negative or no longer useful to you. The following are several techniques for creating a more positive reality: affirmations, symbols and creative visualization or energy projection.

AFFIRMATIONS

Using affirmations enables you to change negative thinking habits into positive ones. An affirmation is a series of positively stated words affirming your health, strength and wisdom. The affirmation is repeated again and again and again while you are in the trance state. To create your own affirmations think of the qualities you wish to affirm in yourself. Then state these qualities as simply as possible. Always state them in the present tense. In this way your unconscious mind understands the goal and will work to bring it about. Say, "I am strong, energetic and competent" rather than "I am going to grow stronger and more competent." The latter puts the situation in the future and the mind won't respond to it. Your power is always in the present. State the affirmation in the positive; otherwise you will be programming yourself in a negative way. Say, "I am wide awake and alert," rather than "I am not sleepy." You may want to write up your affirmation and tape it to your mirror or someplace where you will see it during the day. This is a good means of reinforcement. The following is a list of affirmations that I have found helpful:

"I am a strong, centered and creative woman."
"I will respond only to positive suggestions."
"I have found the inner harmony that flows through me and my body and mind."
"I am surrounded by a circle of loving, supportive energy."
"I am able to focus and direct my energy and do those things I wish to do."
"I am in touch with the calm, expansive power within me."
"I am where I'm supposed to be."
"I am a channel for healing energy."
"I love myself; I am gentle and patient with myself."
"My energies, abilities and confidence are ever-increasing."
"I come from a space of love and abundance."
"I am able to express myself clearly, honestly and directly."

"I am able to release all tensions and resentments."
"I intuitively eat the amount and kind of food necessary to nourish and sustain me."
"All that I need is drawn to me. All that I have I give away. All that I give comes back to me—tenfold."
"There is a golden spirit flowing through me and within that spirit I will live."
"I surrender to the sea of my greater consciousness."*
"I am the creatress of my life."
"All is one and I am one with all that is."
"There is a harmony of season and direction."
"I am reaching deep within the source of my creativity."
"I am in touch with the source of my creativity and originality."
"Inner harmony is the natural state of my being."
"Perfect health is the natural state of my being."
"I am a calm, patient and peaceful woman."
"I dissolve in my mind all feelings of hatred, envy and fear."
"I inhale love, I exhale fear."
"I am open to a flow of energy and guidance in which I will discover the best course of action as I go through each day."
"My priorities in life have become clear to me."
"I will meet those people with whom I can have mutually satisfying and loving relationships."
"I am able to see where I need to direct my energies."
"I am able to deal with my anger openly, honestly and appropriately."
"I use my anger as an agent of transformation."
"I am healthy, wise and loving of myself and others."
"I have the energy, courage and resources to make those changes I need to make."
"Each breath I take brings me closer and closer to a psychic and spiritual awareness."
"I acknowledge, accept and appreciate the wisdom and harmony within myself and within the universe."
"I am open and caring to others and I am able to say those things they need to hear while remaining true to myself and to the greater truth."
"I have a body. I am more than my body. I have a mind. I am more than my mind. I have emotions. I am more than my emotions."
"I am the creatress of my life.
Each thought, each feeling, each belief I hold

---

*affirmation suggested by Sue Silvermarie

Directs the path I take.
I am the creatress of my life.
My inner world of attitudes and emotions
Shapes the outer world of my environment.
I am the creatress of my life.
My thoughts and my dreams
Are the fabrics from which my life is woven.
I am the creatress of my life."

SYMBOLS

The second way of using your thoughts creatively is through the use of symbols. A symbol is an image that represents certain qualities or objects, some of which are unconscious. Symbols help the mind to focus. Suppose you're feeling nervous and spacy. To re-establish your balance, create an image that suggests grounding to you. For example, create in your mind a picture of a tree, its roots planted firmly in the ground. Focus on that tree. If other thoughts try to crowd your mind, let them go and bring your awareness back to the tree. By concentrating on the tree your mind will go beyond it and you'll begin to assume the quality of groundedness symbolized by the tree. In fact, your body will be slowing down, changing vibration. Or suppose you are feeling tired and lethargic and you haven't the energy to do a single thing. Create in your mind's eye the image of a bird, soaring high above the earth. As you concentrate on this bird your body will again change vibration, this time to a higher one, giving you more energy.

You can create symbols for any qualities or situations that you wish to assume. Remember, symbols aren't absolutes. An image symbolizing something to one person may symbolize something entirely different to you. So it's best to create your own symbols.

ENERGY PROJECTION OR CREATIVE VISUALIZATION

The third technique is energy projection, or creative visualization. This is the ability to focus all of your thoughts and images on a specific goal or situation and then project them outward through an effort of will, thus creating the desired effect. Energy projection is done while in the trance state. Having deepened and let go of any worries, fear and pain, you now have a greater concentration of energy at your disposal.

The following is an example of creative visualization: Imagine that you have to move from your current home. Often this can be a difficult and upsetting situation not only because of the scarcity of good housing but also due to the intense emotions that may be connected to the move. In the trance state you have temporarily let these fears go so that you can project positive energy into creating the new situation. Visualize yourself living in the new place. Imagine that you are living there now. Allow yourself to move into the fantasy. Create the scene very vividly in your imagination. Bring up all the feelings and sensations that you would experience if you were actually living there. After five or ten minutes of intense projection return to your usual consciousness. Practicing this exercise will create a buildup of energy that will eventually manifest on a physical level, and you will get that new living space.

We all have negative thoughts and feelings about ourselves as well as patterns of behavior that are no longer useful, yet we keep repeating them. Creative visualization will enable you to change those negative thinking habits. Each time you say, "I'll never find the place I want," or "I'll never be able to afford it," you are setting the scene for failure. You are programming your mind in a negative way. When doing the visualization you are quieting those thoughts, letting them go for the time being and filling your mind with positive thoughts. As you focus on these positive images and project them outward, the energy will begin to take form and your outer situation will eventually change. Remember, you are not repressing your fears: you are releasing them and replacing them with positive thoughts.

Energy projection, the use of affirmations and the use of symbols are all skills that take time and discipline to develop. Our culture gives us many messages of instant gratification, so be aware of this when you are trying these new techniques. You didn't acquire your old habits overnight and it will take more than one night to acquire new ones.

To accept that you are the creatress of your life can be an awesome responsibility, one that you may hesitate to take. Here are some of the stumbling blocks:

1) If you buy the patriarchal "truth" that says something that cannot be proven scientifically doesn't exist, you can become so locked into the physical that anything non-physical will be ignored or completely denied. Living in a technological society demands a very focused kind of awareness in order to produce such a massive array of material goods. Unfortunately, this kind of consciousness has been developed to such an extreme that the diffused kind of awareness that allows you to be in closer touch with the unconscious has been repressed.

2) If you believe that you create your own life and you don't like the circumstances you find yourself in, you feel guilty. People feel guilty whenever they have the experience of deviating, of "missing the mark." Guilt is a part of the force necessary to bring this experience into our conscious

awareness. The feeling of guilt that attaches itself to so many of our experiences is a collective or universal guilt, not just a personal guilt. There is no need to take it upon yourself and act upon it. It is important to learn not to take the guilt literally. (Taking things literally is one of the problems in a society which has overdeveloped the rational.) Realizing the existence of collective guilt is an important step in creating your own reality. First you must acknowledge and accept the feelings; then you must learn to let them go; finally, you will be able to replace the feelings with positive ones.

3) If you are overcome by fear, you are prevented from making connections between inner and outer realities. And there are so many fears: fears of letting go, fears of being judged, fears of the unknown. It is scary to realize that the assumptions, whether good or bad, which have been important in creating who we are may no longer be valid. It is frightening to feel that we will be judged for what we have created, that maybe it isn't good enough or that others won't understand and will think us stupid, slow or immature. And scarier still is the letting go of these fears and beliefs to step into the unknown.

We need to be able to let go of attitudes, beliefs and structures that no longer serve us. Without a process of continual release, we become rigid and unable to grow. Attachments and comparisons belong to the duality of the patriarchy. The female principle is the giver of life, and hence it is also the destroyer. It is the symbol of continual change, the cycle of birth, life, death and rebirth. Fear of letting go, fear of ending, fear of death is the root of woman hating. In releasing these fears, we gain the courage to experiment, to travel without a destination, to have the journey become both the means and the end.

4) If you believe you aren't good enough to get what you want, then those beliefs will block the energy necessary for creative change. Some people think that you shouldn't put too much energy into wishing for something because if it doesn't happen the disappointment will be too great to bear. Working for positive change in your life involves taking risks. The more time spent directing positive energy into change, the more positive changes will occur. And if the change doesn't happen, the time wasn't lost. You were still learning to concentrate. You were affirming that you deserve to get what you want and you were working toward that end. You may learn that you didn't really want what you first thought you wanted. Knowing this and seeing other positive results will lessen the disappointment.

To accept that we create our own reality is a big step to take. It means we must assume responsibility for our own lives. We all have within us a childish part that demands to be loved and cared for, with nothing asked in return. These intense longings, although we don't always act on them or indeed realize consciously that we have them, are always a part of us. Escaping into a religious belief that speaks of a glorious heaven or a blissful nirvana is often easier. So is placing the blame for our misfortunes on other people or on reasons such as unsympathetic parents, lack of money, inferior status as women, bad karma, or adverse astrological influences. These outer influences are real—they place stressful and harmful influences on us—but they aren't everything.

We aren't limited by the physical, material world. We have physical bodies but we are more than physical bodies. We have minds, but we are more than our minds. We have feelings that flow through us but aren't us. We have within us the power to transcend, to transform ourselves. Through the understanding of our inner lives (thoughts, feelings, beliefs) we become centered, and, moving from this clear inner space, we can assume more control (positive direction) over our outer reality.

Don't allow yourself to fall into that trap of egotistical thinking which leads to either of two extreme attitudes: on the one hand, the notion that "I am helpless and cannot protect myself from the forces around me;" on the other hand, the belief that "I am omnipotent and have total control over the forces of nature." It is only through realizing the connection between the inner and outer realities—sensing the ebb and flow of energy—that we are able to walk in step with ourselves, each other and the universe.

It requires time, effort, patience and a lot of self-love to discover and change beliefs, to accept, express and let go our feelings. We must take our dreams and thoughts seriously, treat them with love and respect, and begin to project them outward. The more we realize what we are doing and why we are doing it, the more mindful our actions become and the more control we assume over our own lives. We all carry much unnecessary baggage: worries, fears, guilts, angers, sorrows and pain. Each time we can clear ourselves of this baggage, we move closer to our center, that space of clear understanding and acceptance deep within our psyches. From this inner space, we can create our chosen reality.

We do this each time we learn to rely more on our inner wisdom. Each of us is a multi-dimensional being. Our physical body is but one dimension of the self. On a very deep level we already know all that we need to know. We need to uncover this information, for all learning is really remembering. One of the ways we can tap into the source of our inner wisdom is through conversations with our higher self or Oversoul. This, you remember, is the part of us that has always existed and still exists on the astral plane.

Some people think of this information as coming to us through spirit guides. A spirit guide is an entity existing on the astral plane who chooses to make herself available to people on the physical plane who are asking for guidance. What is thought of as a guide may also be another self, a part of you that exists in another dimension (you in another life), and through trance or meditation or dreams you may reach this self. Whether you visualize this part of you as an Oversoul, Spirit Guide, Ideal Self or different things at different times is not important. What is important is learning to connect with this source of wisdom.

There is only one difficulty I see in conceiving of this inner voice solely as a spirit guide: in so doing you are putting the acquiring of this greater knowledge outside yourself. I believe that it is important for us as women to perceive these revelations as a part of, not as something outside of, ourselves. Taking responsibility for our lives means owning the power that is ours.

When I first became conscious of receiving psychic and spiritual information, I began visualizing my inner self as a higher or ideal self. Then as the presence grew stronger I felt as though it were coming from two guides, entities outside myself. I connected with these guides during meditations and felt good about their advice and presence. Yet I always received this knowledge in my own voice and usually in words that were known to me. (That is, the information seemed consistent with my personal beliefs and experiences.) I began to grow uncomfortable with the thought that what I had considered my intuition was really the voice of another entity. I continued to receive my usual intuitions and continued asking for answers to my personal life in meditation. Gradually the concept of the Oversoul became stronger, especially after two deep trances (which are described in Chapter Seven) in which I asked for specific information about the process of reincarnation. I realized that my Oversoul often manifested itself to me as a glowing light as well as a strong presence. As I continue to seek knowledge I contact both my Oversoul (my higher self) and my spirit guides.

You might want to start a conversation with your Oversoul by asking why it chose to manifest itself in that particular way. Converse with your Oversoul any time you need advice or information. You may want to give your Oversoul a special name, one that you reveal to no other person. When you have a question, pose it in the clearest and simplest form. Make sure you ask only one question at a time. Then relax, deepen and protect yourself. Repeat your Oversoul's name and the question three times. The answer may be sensed or felt; you may see images or hear a voice; it may come later in the day as an intuition or flash or that night in a dream.

Another way to connect with this inner wisdom is through the use of archetypes. An archetype is an inherited, preformed image that is a composite of a certain set of attributes. We have many of these archetypes or characters in our unconscious. One of them is the *Wise Old Woman.*

Wise Old Woman

Relax, deepen and protect yourself. And now let yourself sink deeply into the realm of intuitions, images and archetypes. Deep in this sea of images is the image of a wise old woman. She lives very deeply within you. You may uncover her and enjoy the benefit of her great wisdom. And now you will begin the process of unfolding and opening, of moving toward the old woman and her wisdom, the wisdom of the ages that is unfolding within you.

And now you are at the foot of a mountain. And you begin to climb this mountain, making your way along the stony mountain path. Climbing higher and higher now and the ascent is becoming steeper but you are drawing on an inner strength and the climb is almost effortless. The air is getting thinner now, yet it is clean and clear. And you eagerly make your way upward, almost running the last few steps as you reach the door to the cabin. Here in this cabin lives the wise old woman. She is here to greet you now and you will spend some very important time with her until you hear my voice again. *Pause about ten minutes.*

And now you thank the old woman for her advice and support and you leave the cabin and descend the mountain. Moving down the mountain path and back to your usual waking reality. Return now, relaxed, refreshed and filled with energy. Open your eyes and stretch your body.

Inner wisdom comes from knowing the self. The next two exercises are designed to increase your self-awareness. *Behind the Stage Door* gives you a glimpse of two parts of your personality, two parts that you might find are in conflict. If this is so, you may bargain with these personalities—that is, you may ask each one what it needs and then tell it what you are willing to give to meet that need. Bringing these parts into your conscious awareness makes integration possible and you will have more energy at your disposal. In *Body, Mind and Emotions* you will meet three aspects of yourself and come to know them on a deeper level.

Behind the Stage Door

Relax, deepen and protect yourself. You are fully relaxed now and traveling quickly and easily, floating or flying, flying or floating. You move on and on until you reach an old theater. The lights are dim, there is no one else there. You are alone in that dimly lit theater and you move noiselessly down the aisle, passing row on row of faded, worn leather seats. You take a seat down in the front, not far from the orchestra pit. The orchestra is gone but the memory of the music lingers and you hear it playing faintly.

The curtain is up but the stage is bare. You climb up on the stage and wander across it, turning to face the audience as you sink into reverie. And then you move beyond the stage and enter the door on the left. There seated at the mirrors are two of your personalities. You notice immediately how each is dressed and ask why they are dressed in that way. *Pause about three minutes.*

And you talk to each in turn asking what they need, what they want of you. Each answers you, telling you what they will give to achieve their need. *Pause about five or ten minutes.*

If necessary you will bargain and come to a compromise. *Pause about two minutes.*

And then you leave, walk across the stage once again and back up the aisle. You leave the theater and return to your usual waking reality. Return relaxed, refreshed and filled with energy. Open your eyes and stretch your body.

Body, Mind and Emotions

Relax, deepen and protect yourself. And now as you continue to relax, to float on down, you realize that you are going to a meeting, a very important meeting where you will converse with

three aspects of yourself. This meeting will be held at the top of
a mountain. To carry you to this mountain is a bird, a beautiful
creature, lovelier than any you have seen. And she is here now,
calling you by name and you fly with her to the top of the mountain. *Pause about one minute.*

And now the bird alights on the mountain top and leaves you
there in the quiet and stillness of that cool and airy space. And
here you see your emotions, manifesting themselves before you.
Notice the form they take and talk with your emotions, realizing
that though emotions flow through you, they are not you. *Pause
about three minutes.*

And now, as suddenly as they appeared, your emotions leave.
And again your mind manifests itself before you. Notice the
shape it takes. Talk with your mind, knowing that you have a
mind but you are more than your mind. *Pause about three minutes.*

And now, as suddenly as it appeared, your mind leaves. And
once again another manifestation of you appears, your physical
body. Notice the form it takes and talk with your body, knowing
that you have a body but you are more than your body. *Pause
about three minutes.*

And now, as suddenly as it appeared, your body leaves. And to
your right you see the bird, ready to carry you off the mountain
top. And you fly with the bird up and back to your usual waking
reality. Return relaxed, refreshed and filled with energy. Open
your eyes and stretch your body.

Becoming more powerful means that we learn to rely more on ourselves
to solve problems. It entails learning to trust ourselves and our abilities.
The next exercise is a problem solving technique. To use the exercise, first
think of a problem that you would like to have solved. You will go to a
mind space and look at this problem three different times and in three different ways.

Creative Problem Solving

Relax, deepen and protect yourself. Breathe slowly and deeply, relaxing more and more. And you find yourself walking down
a long, winding staircase, descending on down and around and

around and down. Now you reach a riverbank where a small boat is tied and, climbing aboard that boat, you untie it and sail down the river. It is a warm summer's day. You are enjoying the sun and the breezes on your body as you sail on down the river. Let the rocking motion of the boat and the soothing sound of the water lapping lull you into a dream-like state.

Sailing on now as the day lengthens, the sun climbs higher in the sky and you become warmer and warmer. You anchor the boat and go for a swim. Diving down into the cool water you swim to the bottom and on that river's bottom you see an image, an image of your present problem. Look at that image now. See it clearly and vividly before you. Ask the image why it is showing itself to you in that particular way. *Pause about two minutes.*

And now carry the image back with you as you swim back to the boat. As you come out of the water you realize the image is changing. Sitting on the boat now you carefully observe the image again, asking why it is appearing to you in that way. *Pause about two minutes.*

And now feel yourself lifting up from the boat, floating up into the air, carrying the image of your problem with you. You are floating, flying higher and higher until you reach a cloud. Rest on that cloud and again observe your image and you see that the image has assumed that form. *Pause about two minutes.*

And now the image has dissolved completely and you will return to your usual waking reality, returning with a richer and fuller awareness of your problem. Return now, relaxed, refreshed and filled with energy.

CHAPTER SEVEN

Reincarnation

To write this chapter on reincarnation I asked my friend Cathy who is a member of our mooncircle (a small group of women who meet monthly on the full moon to explore their psychic and spiritual awareness) to guide me into a trance so that I could connect with my higher self. I have had memories of other lives that have come to me in flashes, during meditations, in dreams and trance states, but this time I wanted the help of my higher all-knowing self in exploring how and why we were created.

Although the information I received was not new to me, the feelings while in that altered state were intensely beautiful. Once deepened, I heard a voice saying, "Enjoy yourself: your possibilities are endless." Then it became all feeling and sensation that I translated into words. I was always aware of light, silver light streaming down upon me, and often it was difficult to translate the experience into words. I was engulfed by a feeling of total love, total caring, total unity. The sensations of being born and dying were especially vivid. I felt my body contracting in birth and expanding in death again and again.

Cathy deepened me and then asked me several questions. I have included the transcript here.

Q. Tell me about reincarnation.
A. Reincarnation is the path the soul takes as it moves to rediscover the knowledge that we are all one. There is no within and without. Everything is connected, but we have forgotten that connection.

It's so beautiful. There's so much light. That's what we are: vibrations of light. We are freed by the act of creation. That's what creation is—freedom. We were all created simultaneously by a universal creative energy force and once created, we became creators.

The entity, or soul, is an energy vibration, and that energy is divine. It's like a giant constellation. Each of the stars breaks off as it is created. They are free—whole in themselves—but when they are joined together again they make a greater whole. We are all whole and part of the first creation. We are then sent out to create our own opportunities for learning and exploring. There is a lot of pleasure and excitement in creating. We create as many forms as we can to stimulate our development. This development is going on in all directions, on all levels. It's all light energy, but at different vibrations, different frequencies. It appears to us that only one thing is happening at a time, but that is simply a limitation of the physical body. We have physical eyes and can see what is in front of us but that doesn't mean that what is behind us doesn't exist. It just means that we can't see it unless we turn around. We can transcend that limitation with our minds because the mind is all-seeing. We just don't *know* that the mind is all-seeing, and not knowing is what creates the darkness. Our fears limit us: they block our vision. The more that we realize the extent of our ability to see, the more we *will* see.

Q. How did the world begin?

A. I see a lot of swirling energy—lots of light. Each of these light beams is an entity. It's a whole being; at the same time it's a part of this greater whole.

When you decide to develop something new and test it out, there are different vehicles, different avenues open to you. Before you come into a body, the light is formless. The form limits us, while at the same time it is the form that helps direct us. When we choose to go into a physical body, that body imposes certain limitations on us. The body can become an obstruction if you relate to it only as a physical body. When you begin to realize that it is the mind that creates, then you don't have to be limited by the physical body. If you open the mind, the mind knows, the mind remembers all.

You choose a physical existence to expand your mind, not to be trapped in. Suppose you have three vehicles: a boat, a plane and a car. If you want to travel across or explore the water you take the boat, but you are limited: you can't fly in that boat. You can explore the waters and when you are finished you have to let go of the boat and choose something. You'll choose the airplane to explore the sky or the car to explore the land. Each of those vehicles is for a specific purpose.

Similarly, each of us has chosen a specific form, a specific situation in which to learn, and when our growth and development is completed as much as it can be in that situation, then we must choose another. The more we are able to do that, the more we can integrate.

Sometimes when we come into a body, we become so excited about that physical body that we forget who we really are—bodies of light.

The all-knowing self, the Oversoul, is always present, but when we become so excited about the chosen vehicle, we refuse to hear that inner guiding voice. The knowledge of wholeness is right out there for everyone. We just have to look at it, to notice it, to become aware of it.

The reincarnational process is the journey one sets out upon to discover what one was in the first place.

Q. What is the point of making the journey if you return to the same place?
A. It's for the purposes of exploration, the joy of creating, the joy of discovery and change. The force of love and light is joyful. It's fun to explore and create. Sometimes we become more attached to the creation than to the creator part of ourselves. Our energy becomes blocked, tied to that creation unless we keep returning to the creative source within.

Q. What happens when the entity sheds the physical body?
A. Relief, lightness, freedom. Once the physical body is shed, those limitations are shed with it and everything becomes clearer. Sometimes it is a shock to realize that you are not in the body any more. And the clinging can still persist. Everything doesn't always become clear at once. You have a choice. You can remain attached to the creation, to the product, but that will block you. The more attached you become to the individual products of creation, the harder it is to let go and become aware of the greater whole of creation.

There's such a feeling of serenity here which is so peaceful, so hard to describe. There is so much love.

It's frightening to be born. Dying is letting go, shedding, freeing. Sometimes death is a struggle if you have forgotten that you are the creator and you want to cling to your creations. Dying is like an exhalation. You exhale and the body drops off. You just step out of it and walk away. It's so freeing, so light, so warm. Birth is much harder. You are forced into this tiny form. You feel a struggle to get out. It's so scary that you want to stay in that little space, the womb, yet at the same time you want to get out.

While in the altered state, the most intense feeling I experienced was that of love. I was filled with the awareness that love is the all pervasive life force. It is this loving force that unites us all and is our reason for being. Love is expansive. To love is to grow. It is the absence of fear. Fear is the cause of all suffering, all limitations, all negative emotions. Without fear we can truly learn to give and receive the love we are living for.

I experienced, too, the joy of creation, the realization that we as creators have limitless possibilities. We can grow in as many directions and on as many levels as we wish. Each life is happening now, on a different level or at a different vibration. Each of these parallel souls thus is capable of influencing the other. We have a telepathic connection with our other selves and can contact them through dreams, visions and meditations. The physical self we know now is but one of the many creations of the Oversoul, the total entity that exists on a non-physical plane.

The only way I can describe the Oversoul is as a kind of formless body of light. We probably don't have adequate words to describe the totality of life. We began as that light-being, and we will return to, or rather *as,* that light-being after we fully explore and develop our potential on both material and non-material planes. We are all working towards transcending, changing back into the light-bodies that we were and are originally.

It is important to remember in talking about the process of reincarnation and rebirth that we spring from a timeless universe. Our energy is sent out from our source, core or psyche, and this energy takes different forms on different planes of reality. So that time as we know it is nonexistent. It is all happening now and everchanging, ever circling movement. Our present focus seems to be locked into what we call three-dimensional time: past, present and future. When we dip inward and pull out a portion of that self, we observe it in what appears to be a fixed moment, a small segment of the larger circle. To maintain our equilibrium, our privacy and our physical memories, we see that moment as either past, present or future.

Time is only a way of ordering our experience. It is not really that the past influences the present, but rather that all lives are happening now and are continually influencing each other. So we don't go back in time: we move over; we change vibrations. Our mind creates mental images, and time is the relationship between the images. When we still the mind as we do in deep meditation, the flow of images stops. Hence, time also stops. We exist in the constant or eternal flow.

Many theories of reincarnation view lives in a linear fashion: you did such and such in a past life and because of that such and such is happening to you now. Karma is a complex dynamic involving the molding of past, present and future. We should never reduce it to a simplistic concept of reward and punishment. To do so would be to become dogmatic about the deepest dynamics of human destiny. Karma is the law of action, of change. We can create, and are creating, ourselves at every moment. Our power is in the present. We can cling to a memory from another level, and that memory can affect us in whatever way we choose to let it affect us. But we are not trapped by a difficult past life any more than we are trapped by a difficult childhood. It may often appear that way because of the intensity of the feeling invoked by that memory. Fate is simply the result of our thoughts, feelings and beliefs, and as we change them our fate also changes.

Tapping into other lives, at a time when you can assimilate them, can be extremely helpful. Such information could give you another perspective on your present personality, assist you in discovering hidden talents, help you to understand irrational fears and give you a sense of relatedness and connection to the universe.

We are not aware of all our levels of existence because it would be too much stimulation to handle. We remember as much as we can integrate into our present life. There have been several incidents in my life where recall of other lives has been useful. Ever since I can remember, for example, I have had a fear of dogs that, at times, has assumed irrational proportions. Often, when I am going somewhere I have not been before, I have the fear that I will be bitten by a dog. Last year when I learned that in another life I was killed by a pack of wild dogs one evening when I wandered too far from my village, my fear was greatly lessened. I no longer think dogs will bite me when I go to some place new. The knowledge of that experience along with circles of protection and affirmations has almost alleviated any fear of dogs.

The discovery that my older son was my older brother and the domineering head of the household (our father was deceased) in another life space has enabled me to make our communication clearer at present. Knowing the cause for the confusion in roles has enabled me to set clearer, firmer limits, which have reduced tension considerably. That life took place in Spain, incidentally, a country that I have been drawn to since early childhood.

At another point in my life, when I was developing psychically and spiritually at a very rapid pace, I became afraid that this new awareness would necessitate giving up everything that was important to me: my lover, my family, my home. It was a great relief to realize that in another life where I had concentrated on my spiritual development I had left friends, family and possessions behind to join a monastery in Nepal. In this life, although I am to continue my spiritual development, the form will not be the same. I can draw upon the lessons learned in that life whenever I wish, especially during meditation. That life also explains my intuitive awareness of meditation. I began meditating and teaching meditation without any outer instruction or prior knowledge of it in this life.

How can you stimulate recall of other lives? One method is to ask your dreams for reincarnational information. This is accomplished by giving yourself the suggestion that you will dream about another life space. Repeat the suggestion several times before going to sleep. It may take several nights of suggestion before the dream appears.

Suggestions can also be given during periods of meditation. Affirm to yourself that you will receive insight into other lives. Often this information is close at hand and all you need do is allow yourself to receive it.

Perhaps you are drawn to a particular period of time or a particular country. Maybe you have an instant or intense connection with another person and feel that the relationship must be karmic. Relax and deepen yourself. Then focus on that country, time period or person and suggest that if there are other life connections, the memory will surface now.

Working with a partner, sit facing each other with a candle between you. After deepening ask each other in turn, "Who am I? Who was I? Who will I be?" Watch your partner's face for changes and share them with her.

I have included several exercises which will awaken an awareness of other life spaces. The first exercise in this group is *Revivification of Past Experiences*. This memory exercise allows you to re-experience past, pleasurable events from your present life. People sometimes move spontaneously into other lives while doing this exercise.

All of us at times have felt depressed. During those times it is very easy to remember other hurts, angers or traumas, thus continuing to build on those negative thoughts. Modern psychological theories have placed great emphasis on remembering such painful experiences. It is important to acknowledge such feelings in order to fully release them. It is equally important to learn to uncover and reclaim past feelings of ecstasy, contentment and sensuality. Because thoughts are energy forms and collect similar energy forms, the restimulation of happy experiences will expand your positive energy and create a more affirmative direction in your life. With memory revivification you choose those experiences you wish to respond to, so that you become more conscious and are no longer at the mercy of your emotions or your environment. This exercise also expands your mind by increasing your ability to remember.

You may decide ahead of time which experiences you would like to revivify, or you may relax, deepen and allow your mind to drift back and down, letting memories surface spontaneously. When using the latter method, you need to affirm that only positive memories will surface. It may take a little practice to become able to recall the pleasant experiences. If a negative memory surfaces that you don't want to revivify, you can tell the memory to leave or you can open your eyes.

Revivification of Past Experiences

Relax, deepen and protect yourself. I want you to know that it is possible to go back and down into your past, vividly remembering those experiences that you wish to remember. Going back now, back and down and down and back, to recapture those memories you wish to recapture.

Feel yourself continuing to move back now. Gently carried along by my words, using my words to carry you back and down and down and back. Safely guided by my words, words that carry you back into your past, a past you do want to remember, one that you will remember. Swirling down and around, around and down. Dimly conscious of my words calling you back and down and down and back.

Back to that time and space several years ago that was very pleasant for you, such a pleasant time that you wish to re-experience it now and you will be able to . . . and you are re-experiencing that time and space now. *Pause about two minutes.*

And now, still safely guided by my word, going back and down and down and back. Moving back and down through your life and stopping when you wish to re-experience some happening in this life, something that you very much wish to re-experience, stopping and reliving that experience fully, very fully and vividly experiencing it, yet not so caught up in it that you cannot distinguish it from a present reality. *Pause about two minutes.*

Still moving back now, back and down. If you have not yet begun to experience your body growing smaller and smaller, you will do so now. In that child's body you will experience some childhood happening that was very, very pleasant for you and it is happening again and very fully now. *Pause about two minutes.*

Still very young and growing still younger and younger, you are moving back into that time past and remembering very fully, remembering all those pleasant, happy experiences. *Pause about two minutes.*

And now going back once again or perhaps just continuing to move back to the earliest happy and pleasurable experience you can remember. A memory of being very, very small, perhaps even a tiny baby.

(At this point you may continue moving back into another life, suggesting that you move back farther still, back and back into another time, another life or you may return to your usual consciousness.)

And now hearing my voice calling you back and up, up and back, to the age you were at the beginning of this exercise and bringing with you all those pleasant, happy memories. Knowing that each time you go down and back you will increase your memory and expand your awareness of yourself.

And now you are returning, easily returning. Return wide awake and filled with energy. Open your eyes and stretch your body.

The next five exercises are designed to enable you to experience lives in other dimensions. The first two stimulate a general recall. They are good beginning exercises, and the images are such that you can accomplish the exercises without the help of a guide (the person who deepens you into the trance). The third exercise asks more specific questions and is best accomplished with a guide. It may be done in a group where the participants will be asked certain questions and told that they will remember the answers, or it may be done in an individual session. When experienced individually, the life can be explored in much greater detail since the person exploring will be able to verbalize what she is experiencing. This allows the guide to ask questions that are geared specifically to her responses.

When choosing a guide be sure to pick a person in whom you have confidence. This person should be familiar with trance states. She should know ways of helping people relax, deepen and protect themselves. She should possess the ability to lessen the depth of the trance as well as being able to move someone quickly out of a difficult experience; she should be sensitive and perceptive enough to ask those questions that will promote greater self-understanding. When you are working alone, it is possible to explore karmic ties with a particular person (family member, friend, lover), find reasons for —and ways of working through—irrational fears, uncover hidden talents and find a greater understanding of personality, life goals and beliefs.

The fourth exercise explores what, in linear time, would be a future world, and the fifth exercise uncovers three probable selves. Since all lives are occurring simultaneously at different vibratory rates, it is possible to have several lives during the same time span. In other words, there could be three people living right now who are all a part of your core energy. The fifth exercise, *Through the Looking Glass,* explores these probable selves. This image allows you to uncover multifacets of your own personality or the multidimensions of your being (other living persons that are a part of your total or core energy).

Another Life Space

Relax, deepen and protect yourself. I want you to know that it is possible for you to move over into another dimension, into another life. In just a few moments you will do just that, you will move into another life space and experience a part of that life, something that you would like very much to experience, something that will be important for you to experience now.

And now take a deep breath, a very deep breath and as you fill yourself with air you are becoming lighter, lighter and lighter, so light that you are rising up off the substance beneath you. As you breathe in you are growing lighter, and you are floating in the air, drifting up higher and higher, floating up towards the ceiling and when you reach the ceiling you will exhale and float back down.

And now once again breathe deeply, breathe very deeply and fill yourself with air. Become lighter, lighter and lighter, so light that you are again rising up off the substance beneath you, rising up towards the ceiling. And this time when you reach the ceiling you will exhale and move down and back into another life space. You have reached the ceiling now and as you exhale you will float back and down into another life space. And you will move into that life space now and experience it until you hear my voice again. *Pause about five minutes.*

And now hear my voice calling you back, back to this present life, back to this room. And you will bring back with you those memories of that other life space. You will return now, return easily, wide awake and filled with energy.

Other Life Spaces

Relax, deepen and protect yourself. And now you are settled in the dimension where you can experience your body in any way that you want. And again you find that your body is changing, changing into that of a cat. And in that agile cat's body you climb a tree. Climb up higher and higher, exploring the far reaches of that tree. And now you leap from that tree and find to your amazement that you are not falling but flying higher and higher, flung far out into space.

You are far, far off into space, past all time boundaries so that past is moving into present and present is moving into future and future is moving into past that is also present. And now drifting down, floating down, moving over and into another life space. Move into another life space and experience it now. *Pause about two minutes.*

And now moving up and out of that life space, floating back into space again, away from that life, just letting yourself drift off into space. And once again begin to settle down, to move over and into another life space. Move into and experience another life space. Experience it now. *Pause about two minutes.*

And now moving up and out of that life space. Floating back into space again. Away from that life, just letting yourself drift off into space. And now drifting down, floating down, moving over and into another life space. Move into and experience another life space. Experience it now. *Pause about two minutes.*

And now moving up and out of that life space, floating back into space again, away from that life, just letting yourself drift off into space. And once again begin to settle down, to move over and into another life space. Move into and experience another life space. Experience it now. *Pause about two minutes.*

And now moving up and out of that life space, floating off into space again, skimming freely along until you decide which of those lives you wish to experience more fully and then you will move into that space. Choose that life now and move into it again and experience it more fully now. *Pause about five minutes.*

And now hear my voice calling you back to your present reality, back to this room. Return at your own pace. And return feeling wide awake and filled with energy. Open your eyes and stretch your body.

Past Life Regression

Relax, deepen and protect yourself. And now stretch out through the soles of your feet. Stretch on out about three feet and then come back to your usual size and relax. And now stretch out through the top of your head, stretch on out about three feet and then come back to your usual size and relax. And now stretch out through your right side. Stretch on out about three feet and then come back to your usual size and relax. And now stretch out your left side. Stretch on out about three feet and then come back to your usual size and relax. And now stretch out all over, through your feet, through your head, through your sides. Stretch and expand so that you fill the room. And you are very light and very free. Enjoy it awhile and then come back to your usual size.

And now I want you to realize that all of us carry with us attitudes, beliefs and feelings from other life spaces. And sometimes these can become an impediment to our progress in our present life space. And by remembering them we can work to release them, and in fact sometimes the knowing is also the releasing. And I want you to realize also that all of us carry within us hidden talents and unrealized potentials. We carry these over from other life spaces. The good is never lost. And in remembering the good we become fuller, richer and more aware.

In just a few moments I'm going to ask you to move into another life space but for now I want you to move to the top of this building. Move to the roof of the building and look down at the street below. Notice and remember all that you see. And now float up higher, find yourself floating or flying high above the earth, flying higher and higher, enjoying the sense of freedom and lightness. *Pause about one minute.*

And now I'm going to ask you to drift back and down to earth again, drift back and down and into another life space. Return to earth in another life space. I'm going to count from ten to one and by the time I reach the count of one you will have touched down on earth again and in another life. *Count.* You are standing on the earth again. Look down at your feet and notice what, if anything, you are wearing on your feet. And now your legs, your body, what are you wearing, how are you dressed? Are you a woman or a man? Notice and see clearly. Look around you now and become aware of the space you are in. Outdoors or indoors? Alone or with others? Be fully aware of who you are and where you are. Know what you are doing there. *Pause about three minutes.*

And now still in that body and in that life I'm going to ask you to move to the time when you were about five years old. Move to that time and experience it or see it clearly before you. Go to the space where you live. See it clearly and be able to describe it in detail. *Pause about two minutes.* And see now the people you live with. See them clearly and vividly. And you remember your feelings and your thoughts about them. *Pause about two minutes.* And now see your parents, see them very vividly and feel their vibrations. Feel them strongly and know if you know them in your present life. *Pause a minute.*

And now move to an important experience in that life. Move into it and remember it. *Pause about two minutes.*

And now move into another experience, an important experience. *Pause about two minutes.*

And again move into another important experience. *Pause about two minutes.*

And now aware that you are fully protected, very fully protected, move to your death day. See it clearly. *Pause about a minute.*

And now leave your body. You have left your body. You are moving into your higher consciousness, moving into your higher consciousness and able to look at that life you just experienced. Look at it and know what lesson you learned in that life. *Pause a minute.* And still looking at that life, know what you carried from that life into your present life. *Pause about a minute.*

And now let go of that life, let go of those experiences, yet remember them in a way that is comfortable for you. Leave that life and travel back to your present reality, your own awareness and identity completely restored. And you will return relaxed, refreshed and filled with energy. Take your time and then open your eyes and stretch your body.

Future World

Relax, deepen and protect yourself. Feel yourself now to be drifting off into space. Drifting along into the far, far reaches of space. And feeling your body growing, growing to a size so immense that you could conceive of yourself as a giant constellation of stars.

You are drifting off into space and your body assuming the size and shape of a giant constellation. You are the Goddess Diana, the Huntress. And as Diana, you raise your arm to shoot an arrow. The arrow flies off into the air, speeding through the night. And soon you find that you are also that arrow, a shooting star, traveling through time and space. A tiny, tiny cell. A microcosm where once the macrocosm was. A tiny cell yet aware of your whole body and all the harmonious inter-relationships within you. Wise and knowing, all knowledge within, centered in this tiny cell.

And now this tiny cell, this arrow spins off into space, spinning off into that space we call future. Feel your consciousness expanding now, expanding as it descends into that future space. A different reality, one that you have never known, yet one that you have always known. This is the world of the future that you and all strong women are creating. And it is here now, and you are here. *Pause five minutes.*

And now hear my voice calling you back, back to this room, back to your present life. Back, come back now. Come back wide awake and filled with energy. Open your eyes and stretch your body.

Through the Looking Glass

Relax, deepen and protect yourself. Turn away from the outer world, away from its noise, away from its tensions, away from its distractions. Turn away from the outer world and its concerns.

These things no longer concern you as you continue to become more and more relaxed.

Here in this calm and serene space you will be able to experience the multidimensions of your personality. Here in this space you will meet your probable selves. Here in this space you will have an awareness that transcends your usual three-dimensional reality.

It is in this space now that you find yourself looking into a mirror, a three-framed mirror. And as you look into the first frame of the mirror your gaze moves beyond and through the looking glass and you see coming toward you another self, a probable self. Step into that looking glass now and become that self, experiencing that self. *Pause about five minutes.*

And now move gently back and away from that probable self. You are back into your own body again and facing the mirror, the second frame of the mirror. And looking beyond and through the looking glass you see another probable self coming toward you. Step through the looking glass and become that self, experiencing that self. *Pause five minutes.*

And now move gently back and away from that probable self. You are back into your own body again and facing the mirror, the third frame of the mirror. And looking beyond and through the looking glass you see another probable self coming toward you. Step through the looking glass and become that self, experiencing that self. *Pause five minutes.*

And now move gently back and away from that probable self. You are back in your own body again and facing the three-framed mirror. Facing the mirror and seeing at once all three probable selves. And now watch as those images fade. Let those images fade but remember very vividly all that you have experienced.

And once again drift up and back to your usual waking reality. Drift back at your own pace and return wide awake and filled with energy.

I wanted to conclude this chapter with some specific information concerning what happens when the physical body is shed and the astral body moves onto the astral plane. In other words, what happens when you die? I asked my friend Cathy to help me deepen and move into my higher consciousness. Cathy did so and then asked me what exactly happens at death. I experienced a sense of peace which was so relaxing I didn't really want to speak, although it was easier this time than the last. At all times I was aware of a group of light beings who surrounded me. I felt absolute peace. I felt that I was being shown, often in symbols, what occurred after death. Examples were given, mostly in picture form, of things I had encountered on the earth that would most closely represent what occurs on the astral plane. I always had the sense that much, much more happened on the astral plane, but that I was being shown only the very first level. The words I formed never quite seemed to explain the experience. Although I described other lives in linear terms, I was aware that I did that for ease of description and not because of the way it happened. I sensed that it was occurring now, and to signify it I was shown only one small portion of the entire happening. There are many other levels of vibration, of life, that I am not yet equipped to see. Yet I sensed more, and once I saw an even higher being, who was so dazzlingly bright I could not completely focus my gaze on it.

Q. What happens when you die?
A. When the body dies it slowly shuts down. The heart stops, the breathing stops, the brain stops, the organs stop functioning. Everything gradually trickles away. The astral body oozes out, leaving your body from a spot a little below the navel. It forms a cloud. Remember the pictures of Aladdin and the lamp. When he rubbed the magic lamp a hazy cloud formed first and, as the cloud thickened, it gradually shaped into the genie. Well, that's how the astral leaves: a little cloud gets thicker, thicker and thicker, finally takes shape and leaves as the silver cord just dries up, just like a baby's umbilicus. And then you float off.

What happens to you immediately after leaving the physical body is whatever you think is going to happen. If you have an awareness that death is merely a transformation, a rebirth—which is what it is—you die to the physical world and are reborn to the astral, you rejoin your friends and teachers there. I see a picture of a person just stepping over a threshold. Just a small step and figures are waiting there; they take your hand and help you step over.

But if you think that nothing happens to you when you die then you stay in that nothingness for a while. It's sort of a cold, black haze, and you remain there until it dawns on you that you are still alive, you can still move around, you are still thinking. You start to move around, and, as you notice your movement, the cloud seems to lighten. The other entities are on the fringes, waiting to tell you where you are when you are ready to know. Nobody tries to force you. No one rushes through the cloud and shakes you saying, "Wake up." They wait until you come around.

When you are in the astral plane your thoughts manifest instantly. There isn't the time lapse, the limitation such as on the earth plane, where it takes much discipline and concentration to manifest something. Whatever you think is going to surround you does. You can stay in that space creating thought forms as long as you want, until you finally get bored with it. Then, whatever you have created with your thought forms fades away as you withdraw your energy from it. Then, when you are ready, there are entities waiting to explain what it is all about.

It's a very peaceful feeling. There's almost a golden glow. It's total acceptance. No one is there laughing at you. Each person is understood to be an individual who will create whatever is needed. Guides are there to help, guides who have that job as their special occupation. Some entities work specifically with people who have just crossed over.

Then there is a period of sleep, of varying degrees, depending on your needs. If you had a lengthy illness before you died, you may need time to recover from it.

Once you realize where you are and accept that you really aren't dead, but have slept and got yourself back together again, you go to your hall of memories. (It seems that I'm being shown this in symbols.) I get a picture of a huge room. I can connect it with that theater at Disney World where

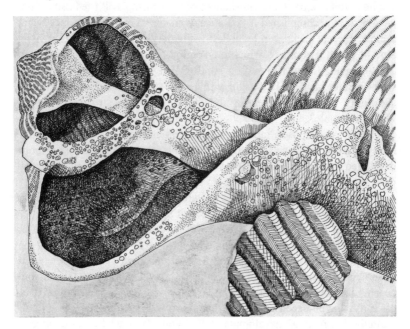

the movie screen circles the whole theater and you stand in the middle. Here you remember all that has happened to you. You see not just your most recent life, but all your lives. You become aware of what your soul's purposes are. It seems that space is the first of many schools that you attend on the astral plane. You go there and restimulate your memory. You realize why you chose to incarnate at that particular time, what your purposes were, what your accomplishments were, the ways in which you grew and expanded and the ways in which you limited yourself. You judge yourself, "grade" yourself. You have full awareness of yourself and your abilities.

The next step is to decide how you can best further your development. Are you going to move back into the earth's plane to do it? (I see a lot of light-beings.) There are very many planes. You have to proceed at your rate. There are some planes that even on that astral level are too vast to understand. When you pass over, you remember everything about yourself. You know a lot, much more than you knew on the earth plane, but you don't know everything.

You have to reach a certain level of development to choose the circumstance of your birth in a more careful, conscious way. (I can see beings standing in the background.) You can have all the help you want. There are beings who have experienced more than you at this point and therefore can help you decide the circumstances of your birth. Will the lessons you need be best accomplished if you are a woman or a man? What race, what socio-economic background will best facilitate your development? Which kind of family grouping? Which time period is best? Everything is chosen. Are you going to live in a nuclear family? Will your mother be someone who does not have a relationship with a man? Will you be given up for adoption? Will you choose a family where you all have strong ties and are very compatible? Or will you choose one with strong ties but much conflict? Will you choose a family who is interested more in education or one motivated just by survival? A family which is spiritual or one that is more developed in material ways? Will you choose a family that is quite developed in some aspect that you wish to pursue or one whose interests seem in opposition to yours? Or will it be a grouping that's pleasant but loosely connected, leaving you free to form a different primary focus?

You also choose the cycle of life. Will it be a very brief stay or a longer one? Will you be able to see to completion some of your tasks, or will they be stopped abruptly by your death? Is your purpose to carry on the work of someone before you, or to have others who will carry on the work you began? Do you feel you need to learn a lesson by having your potential cut off early, maybe because you have been involved in situations where you inhibited other people's development? Will you have your life terminated early to recreate the balance? Some people doggedly stick to one particular task, which they return to again and again in different circumstances. Often those people are what we call geniuses or child prodigies. Other people scatter their development in many directions. Some people choose very dramatic or difficult circumstances to heighten their development.

Q. How does this relate to the Oversoul?

A. The entity on the physical plane is but one aspect of the total energy of the Oversoul. It is possible while on the earth plane to become more aware of your purposes. You can become more aware of them by realizing the existence of your Oversoul. You can contact your Oversoul through dreams, meditation and guided fantasy. Actually, when you pray you are sending your request out to your Oversoul. When you do creative visualization, you are sending that energy out to your Oversoul also. The more that you can focus your energy, the clearer you become. In a sense it will be easier for you to achieve your goals. You can have more of a balanced attitude when you have a sense of the larger picture. You don't get tied into or blinded by your own personal viewpoint as often. Communicating with your Oversoul is like allowing yourself to step back and view the whole situation. You realize that there are unseen purposes and unseen forces.

Q. What is the connection between Oversouls on the astral plane?

A. I see huge beings of light with hands spread out, and from their hands, rays of light that connect them to all other smaller beings. Then all the smaller beings are gathered up into the Oversouls and all the Oversouls are turned and folded together like a flower forming one large being, like a giant constellation. All together the Oversouls are the whole of creation, that total energy. The Oversoul is the sovereign body. In the beginning when the entities were all created simultaneously, each entity was an Oversoul who, freed by creation, created more forms to carry out individual explorations. Each smaller entity is a part of the creation of the Oversoul and each Oversoul is a part of the exploration and creation of the Goddess.

I can see a picture of all the dimensions. It's like a huge hand holding many mesh screens. And the screens can fan out—become different dimensions—or fold together, mesh as one. Each mesh screen is an arena, stage, or life space, and each has a slightly different tempo, beat or vibration. That's where you get the idea of time. It seems as though one screen or time is 42-2000 B.C., another 1500 A.D. or 2000 A.D., because everything is lived out at a different rate of vibration. As in the animal kingdom where a flea might live twenty-four hours, something else lives three days, another a week, three months, seven years, and so forth. Yet each animal goes through its total life span in whatever allotted time it has. The ones with the shorter time span move at a faster vibration.

Q. How does the astral plane relate to the earth plane in terms of time?
A. It's a different level of vibration. I think that's where the concept of heaven and hell came in, because there are different levels of vibration. There isn't a heaven or hell in the Christian sense, but there are different stages of growth. Just like different musical notes. I see a big symphony— I hear the symphony. There can be discord. It's all movement. That's what life is, movement. A flow back and forth, ebb and flow, wax and wane. That's what creates movement. Like breathing, there has to be both inhalation and exhalation. Batteries must have both positive and negative poles. Just like a magnet's north and south. The earth is a big magnetic field. There is a way to move out of that field. In the astral plane you move outside of the magnetic field.

Q. Is there a positive and negative on the astral plane?
A. Not on higher planes. I don't know how you have that movement without the tension, but it feels different. Maybe that's why it is so peaceful, the tension isn't there, but the movement is. Different laws operate there. There is no law of gravity.

CHAPTER EIGHT

Dreams

Dreams are messages from your psyche *about* your psyche. Remembering, recording and reflecting on your dreams enable you to reach a deeper understanding of yourself. Dreams try to give you knowledge of your hidden talents and unused creative energies, as well as knowledge of the negative, neglected or repressed parts of your personality.

Dreams have a reality different from, but no less valid than, the physical reality. At times they seem to weave a hazy thread so elusive you can't quite grasp it, and at other times they portray events so vividly that you are shocked into recognizing something that has been consciously unknown to you. Dreams magnify and intensify feelings in order to bring them to your attention.

Dreams can enrich your life by opening up many new possibilities for you. They are repositories for both your personal unconscious (your forgotten memories, unrealized talents, repressed desires, basic instincts and creative energies) and the collective unconscious (the inherited wisdom of humankind, that dimension where we are all connected with the universal mind.) It is through the understanding of your dreams that you can reconnect your feelings to your thoughts, and your body/mind to universal spiritual forces.

In your dreams you work out problems, release hostilities and fears, identify solutions and feelings that you were not aware of in your waking life. This is possible because your dreaming mind is free of the social, cultural and political biases of your waking mind and is therefore able to pick up feelings and vibrations that have been overlooked. Your dreams are created from the realm of timelessness, where past, present and future are one. Freed from the illusion of linear time, dreams bring you messages from the past (both past memories and past incarnations), show you what is happening in the present and allow you to see into future events and possibilities.

A dream brings you messages from many dimensions. Here in your dreams you can connect with your Oversoul, glimpse another incarnation and gain information about other people, places or events. Each of these occurrences must be interpreted in light of your present situation as well. Such things are being revealed to you now because there is a direct relationship to your immediate situation.

Dreams speak to you in pictures and images, using symbols that are at once universal and uniquely your own. You cannot separate the symbol from the dream or the dream from the dreamer. To understand your dreams you must give them the attention and respect they deserve. You must hold them dear to you, turning them over and over in your heart, establishing a dialogue with them until the message becomes clear. In learning to understand the language of dreams, you may look to the universal symbolism of myths and fairy tales, or incorporate the insights of other people, but only the dreamer herself can say, "This is the meaning that rings true for me."

Dream Recall. To remember your dreams give yourself the suggestion, "I will remember my dreams," and repeat it several times before falling asleep. The suggestion will be more easily absorbed if you relax and deepen first. Have a pen and paper next to your bed so you can write down your dreams on awakening. This also serves to let your dreaming self know that you really want to remember your dreams.

Re-enter the Dream. Relax, deepen and protect yourself. Imagine that you are walking down a long, winding staircase and when you reach the bottom you will step into your dream. Continue the dream to completion and then return to your usual reality.

Meditate on a Dream Symbol. Choose a symbol from one of your dreams that is not clear to you. Now relax, deepen and protect yourself. Travel to your mind space, see the symbol and rest quietly, allowing the images and realizations to arise. You may find it helpful to give yourself the suggestion that when observing the symbol more images will arise which will increase your understanding and make the meaning clear. Before returning to your usual awareness, suggest that further insights will come to you throughout the day.

Dialogue with a Dream Character. Choose a character from one of your dreams that you would like to learn more about. Relax, deepen and protect yourself. Travel to your mind space, telling yourself that when you arrive there your dream character will appear. See the character vividly before you.

Now have a dialogue with the character asking why she appeared in your dreams and what she can teach you. When the conversation is finished return to your usual reality.

Request Dreams About Specific Problems. Now that you are remembering and reflecting on your dreams, you might want to begin requesting specific dreams. You can work out anger, resentment, fear, anxiety or any difficulty by requesting dreams for that specific purpose. For example, if you are having difficulty acting independently, ask for dreams in which you are behaving in an independent way. Repeat this request several times before going to sleep. Or, if you have trouble expressing your anger, ask for dreams in which you express your anger without hurting yourself or anyone else. It may be necessary to use these suggestions for several consecutive nights.

Find Solutions to Problems. Give yourself the suggestion that you will have a dream in which the solution to a particular problem will appear. State the suggestion clearly and simply and repeat it several times before going to sleep. It may take several nights of suggestions before you have the solution dream.

Find Your Innermost Thoughts and Feelings. If you are unclear about how you really feel about something, give yourself the suggestion that you will have a dream which will reveal your true feelings. Repeat this suggestion several times before going to sleep. It may take several nights of suggestions.

The following series of exercises are guided fantasies designed to take you into the dream space. *Womanvision* is a fantasy for women to explore their inner space, their bodies, their images and their dreams. *The Knowing Dream* allows you to move safely into a dream space where you will be able to view yourself and your life as you have created it. In so doing you will have a new awareness of yourself and bring that awareness back to your everyday reality. In *Temple Sleep* you will re-enact an ancient healing rite, that of going for a night into a temple or sacred space. While in that space, you will fall into a deep dreamlike sleep, and during this sleep Goddesses and other entities will visit you and do whatever is necessary to effect a healing. *Inner Journey* is a call to travel. You may travel deep within your dreaming space, or you may leave your physical body and travel in your astral body wherever you wish.

The Marshland Ritual is based on my friend Kata's dream in which she enters a marshland where a ritual is about to be performed. She is privileged to witness this ritual so that she may gain knowledge. At the time of the dream Kata, myself and several other women were celebrating full moon rituals. After her dream Kata wrote a fantasy and put it on tape so we could all move into trance and experience the ritual.

Womanvision

Relax, deepen and protect yourself. And now you are very still, very relaxed and listening to your body/mind. Let your energy flow as you come into very close touch with your body/mind. Become aware of all the sensations in your body as you continue to relax and let your energy flow.

Feel yourself sinking very deeply into your womanbody. Feel yourself totally centered in your womanspace and have a total awareness of your woman's body and feel it very deeply and become aware of your muscles and tendons, aware of the very marrow of your bones.

Become aware of your legs and feet. And feel the strength in your legs and feet. Aware of your woman's body, aware of your pelvic area, your womb, aware of your life force, aware of your woman's body, aware of your abdomen, aware of every cell and tissue, aware of all the tissues and organs, aware of your strengths, aware of your empty spaces, aware of your fullness. Have a total awareness of the cells and tissues in your body, aware of your chest and breasts, aware of your strength, aware of your softness. Have a total awareness of your woman's body, aware of your back, aware of each vertebra, aware of the muscles and tendons in your back, aware of your strengths, aware of your limitations, aware of your shoulders and neck, the muscles, the tendons, the bones. Aware of your woman's body, aware of your arms and hands, aware of your energies, your powers, your creativity. Aware of your woman's body, aware of your head, fully aware of your mind, your strength, your wisdom, aware of your eyes, your nose, your mouth, your lips, your cheeks, your ears, your scalp. Totally aware of your woman's body and your woman's strength.

And now let that awareness of your body fade. Let it gradually and easily fade as you move deeper and deeper within your womanspace. Sinking very deeply into your womansoul. Aware only of your consciousness now, feeling very light and very free, your body is very light and the awareness of it is fading, fading. Your awareness is total womanconsciousness. Feel yourself to be totally centered within your womanspace. And now you begin to dream. In fact you have never ceased dreaming. And you are dreaming that dream onward, dreaming, carrying onward that woman's dream. And your vision blurs to a wider focus as you surrender to the sea of your greater consciousness, and swimming in that sea of shared imagery you dream. Dreaming, swimming, floating, dreaming. Womanspace, womansoul, womandream. *Pause five or ten minutes.*

Swimming upward now, carrying the dream, bringing the womandream up and back. Swim up and back to your usual waking reality. And return relaxed, refreshed and filled with energy. Open your eyes and stretch your body.

Knowing Dream

Relax, deepen and protect yourself. And now you are fully relaxed and very deeply in trance. You find yourself in a desert. Coming towards you is a magnificent horse. You climb astride that horse and gallop off across the desert sands. The horse's movements are so graceful and swift it seems that the horse's legs are your legs and you and the horse are one. And you gallop on and on, almost flying across the desert sands.

And now you come to rest at a small, cool and green oasis. Here in the midst of the oasis is a beautiful tent, a silken tent with golden bells jingling at the entrance. And you climb down from the horse and walk to the entrance of the tent, but you are unable to enter because the tent is filled, completely filled, with people, with things and with feelings. The tent is so cluttered that you could not possibly enter. And while you stand there amazed at that clutter, a strong gust of wind blows through the tent, and takes with it all that clutters the tent. The wind has swept through the tent and it is empty save for a single richly textured rug in the center of the tent. The symbols are so intricate in this tapestry that it feels as though they are magic. And magic they are, as you lie on that rug and feel the comfort and protection those symbols offer. And protected by those symbols you drift safely off into a warm dream-like sleep. And moving into this dream, dreaming this dream, swimming safely in your dream, you are able to see your life. You see your life, clearly and vividly, as you form it. And looking through the dream you can see those parts of your life you wish to see, knowing that you can accept both the painful parts and the joyful parts, for they are all a part of you. And looking now at your life, safely protected by the magical symbols woven on that rug, you will come to a new and clearer understanding of who you are, where you have been and where you are going. You will see this with an awareness not ordinarily accessible to you in your usual waking reality. Yet when you have this dream you will become clear and bring this clarity back to your usual waking reality. *Pause five or ten minutes.*

And now waking from that dream and carrying that dream with you up and back to your usual waking reality. Dream the dream onward and return relaxed, refreshed and filled with energy. Open your eyes and stretch your body.

Temple Sleep

Relax, deepen and protect yourself. Your breath is becoming slower and slower, moving lower and lower. And now become aware of the wind, hear the rush and hum of the wind. Feel the breezes sweep over your body. Let the wind sweep through your mind, clearing it of all thoughts, sweeping away all fears, all pain, all anger, all doubt. Let the strong clean wind sweep over you and carry you deep into the recesses of your soul, deep, deep into the recesses of your psyche. Let the wind carry away all your strain, all your tension, all your confusion.

And you are clean and clear now, feeling very light as you float down and down, protected as always with a circle of light that enfolds you and keeps you from all harm.

And now you are entering a very deep dreamlike sleep during which you will experience, like ancient women, a ritual of healing, a ritual of regeneration, a ritual of rebirth.

And now remember how our foremothers would separate themselves from the rest of the villagers and go to the temple of the Goddess. And during the night Goddesses and other entities would come to them to do whatever was necessary for their healing and rebirth. The Goddesses would appear in a dream, a vision, a sparkling intuition, and serve as a catalyst to awaken energies that would continue to flow long after the women awoke.

And like these ancient women you will now move on deeper and deeper until you find yourself in a beautiful temple, a temple beyond the reaches of time, a temple contained in a sacred space. And here in this sacred space you will be greeted by hooded and robed figures, figures whose faces are lost in the shadows.

Follow these figures now as you wind through the long corridors, winding through the labyrinth of time. Winding down and around until reaching the center space, a circular space which contains only a single slab of stone. And here, upon this stone, you will lie like the women of old and have a dream—a dream of healing, a dream of renewing, a dream of rebirth. *Pause about ten minutes.*

And now awakening from that dream you will rise up from that stone and move back along the long winding corridors. And as you slowly make your way, you are moving up and back to your usual waking reality. Take your time and remember all that you have experienced. And when you return you will open your eyes and stretch your body.

Inner Journey

Relax, deepen and protect yourself. You are relaxing now, breathing deeply and becoming more and more relaxed. Each breath is carrying you deeper, deeper and deeper. These journeys are taken with one purpose in mind, to bring you into a deeper awareness and understanding of yourself. To know and to love that self and to realize, if you have not already realized, that you are more than your physical body, that you perceive more than your ordinary senses perceive, that you know more with your mind than its logical thought knows. You are more than your physical body, more than your logical mind, more than your experiences.

And you can understand all this and understand it fully as you learn to travel in many dimensions. Travel into spaces where you are free of your physical body, free of your thoughts, free of your fears, free of your pain, free of your anger, free of your worries. You can leave them all behind, as you are leaving them now and responding to my voice. And now see beside you an old black trunk, with leather handles and big brass hinges. Lift the heavy lid of that trunk now and place within it all your worries, fears, pain, anger and envy. Leave all your sorrows and fears behind. Just put them in the trunk and then close the heavy lid. *Pause about one minute.*

And now hear my voice calling you to leave this material world. And know that although you are leaving your physical body behind, it will remain safely in this room and you may return to it whenever you wish, but for now you will leave it behind and begin to travel.

You are beginning a journey, a gentle journey, a journey of self-love and self-awareness, a journey in which you will begin to explore the self that existed before the self you now call by your name, a journey where you will come to know and trust yourself and the many dimensions of your self. Begin to travel now, easily and gently out and away from your physical body. You may travel wherever you wish and then in a little while I will call you back, back into this room, back into your physical body, but for now you will travel freely, easily and safely, on this journey of self-love. Travel and remember, remember all that you experience. *Pause about seven minutes.*

And now become aware of my voice again, calling you back, back into this room and back into your physical body. Return easily and gently and be relaxed, refreshed and filled with energy.

Marshland Ritual

Relax, deepen and protect yourself. Travel to a forest and wind your way through the forest, going deeper and deeper, down and down. And following along that forest path you notice the earth becoming softer beneath your feet. The air has grown cool and moist, the earth soft and spongy. Soon you have entered a marsh and this marshland awakens within you memories of a far distant past. Remember now, and the memory is vivid, this is the place where your sisters gathered each month when "the moonswell fills to brimming." *

And they are here again tonight and you eagerly join them, moving swiftly into their circle. You enter their circle knowing that together you will participate in a ritual to gain knowledge. Together, hands joined, you circle, slowly at first, circling round and round. Swaying and circling in the moonlight, humming a quiet chant. Round and round you go as the circle begins to move faster and faster. Your whole body in motion now, gentle, strong motion.

Your voices chant full and rich. The chanting and dancing become stronger, louder and faster. The ritual of knowledge has begun. Knowledge, intuitive knowledge will be gained in extraordinary ways.

And as you continue swirling and turning in the moonlight, your body begins to change. All the women's bodies are changing, changing into those of geese. And suddenly the flock of geese soars off into the night, off to gather knowledge. Upon returning to the marshland you will again assume your own form, your own body, but now in the bodies of geese you will gather knowledge. *Pause about ten minutes.*

And now hearing my voice calling you back, back to the marshland, back to your own body, your own identity completely restored. And now return to this room, return wide awake and filled with energy, carrying with you the knowledge that is yours.

*Sue Silvermarie, "Meeting" in *Letters of a Midwife.*

CHAPTER NINE

Psychic Skills for Children

Encouraging the development of psychic awareness in children is a rewarding and enjoyable endeavor. Children naturally strive toward growth and life. They are extremely curious; with their vivid imaginations they move easily into imaginary worlds. Children are eager to tell their dreams, and your interest further stimulates their dream recall. Since their awareness has not yet been limited by rational, logical thought, they accept their dreams as real and important. Unfortunately, this spontaneity is often crushed and children are admonished to stop telling tales, to stop daydreaming. Developing psychic skills teaches them to relax and remain centered in their own bodies, to listen intensely, to see intensely and to appreciate and respond to their dreams. It teaches them to use their imagination and their daydreams to create the situations they want. It shows them positive ways of releasing feelings and places value on being in touch with their emotions and intuitions. They learn to become more independent, to rely on themselves rather than learning to manipulate adults into gratifying their desires.

My household includes two adults and three children, Mike, Marc and Jake. I began working with the kids when they were 5, 6 and 8 years old. We started with relaxing and breathing exercises done each night before bedtime. Instead of hearing the usual bedtime story, the kids lay down with their eyes closed and I guided them into trance and took them on a fantasy trip that ended with "and you will remember what you did and tell me in the morning."

Deep Relaxation

Let's see if you can relax your body just like when you are
sleeping, but you will stay awake and be able to hear what I am
saying. Lie down and get comfortable. Now close your eyes and
begin to relax your body as I talk. Wiggle your toes and feet and
then let them relax. Let them go loose and limp like Raggedy Ann
or Raggedy Andy. Now let your stomach relax. Let it become
very loose, like you are filled with sawdust. Now squeeze your
hands together, make a fist and then let your hands relax. Now
squeeze your eyes real tight and now let them relax. Your whole
body is very relaxed now. You are just like a Raggedy Ann, loose
and limp. Your body is filled with sawdust.

Deep Breathing

Take a great big breath now and let it out, pushing that breath
as far as you can. Pretend that you are blowing your breath across
the world. Now take another deep breath, pull in all that air. And
now let all that air out very slowly, pushing it across the world.
Keep breathing very slowly now. Pull all that air in and then push
it all the way across the world. Put your hands on your stomach
and feel it move in and out as you breathe. Pretend you are blowing up a giant balloon and then let all the air out of the balloon.
Pause about one minute. This breath is coming deep from within
the center of your body. You have a lot of energy and you can
learn to use it in many ways. Feel the energy moving in and out
as you breathe in and out. This is your life energy. It keeps you
alive, strong and well. Open your eyes now.

Intense Listening

(Children may be lying down or sitting for this exercise.)
Let's see if you can learn to listen with your inner ear. Close
your eyes and get very comfortable. Let your body relax just like
we've done before. Make each part of your body get very loose,
as if you were filled with sawdust. (Continue with further guided
relaxation if necessary.)

Now take a great big breath, pulling in lots of air, and then let
it out slowly as if you were pushing it across the world. Keep
taking big breaths and slowly pushing out the air, pushing it to the
end of the world.

Listen now to the sounds your body is making as it breathes in
and out. Maybe your stomach is grumbling a little. Maybe you
can hear or feel your heartbeat. Maybe you hear or feel a vibration, a shaking in your body. Listen very closely to the sounds
your body makes. Hear only the sounds of your own body. *Pause
about one minute.*

Now listen very, very closely to the sounds around you, the
sounds outside your body. Listen to all the sounds outside your
body and remember what they are. Listen to all the soft sounds,
the tiny noises outside your body. (Mention the sounds around
you.)

Now keep your eyes closed and begin to shut out the sounds
around you. Close out all those sounds. Listen again only to the
sounds in your body. Listen only to your body. Listen to your
breathing. Listen to your heartbeat. Listen to your stomach
grumbling.

Now open your eyes. Did you hear differently than you usually
do? Were you able to shut out outside sounds and listen only to
your body? What sounds did you hear first when you began to
let the other sounds in? Could you hear soft sounds that you don't
always hear when you are playing? Could you go back to listening
only to your own sounds?

Intense Seeing

Sit down so that you feel very comfortable. Now close your eyes and let your body relax. (Continue with further guided relaxation if necessary.)

Now take three deep breaths. Breathe in, hold your breath and now blow the air out through your mouth as if you were blowing out a candle. And now do it again, breathe in, hold your breath and let the air out through your mouth as if you were blowing out a candle. Good. Now breathe like that once more.

Now open your eyes and look at this picture (or object that you have chosen beforehand). Look at it very closely. Now close your eyes and see if you can describe that picture to me. Tell me everything you remember. Now open your eyes and look at the picture again. Were you able to remember everything about the picture? Now stand up and walk slowly around the room. Look very carefully. Your eyes are like cameras, taking pictures of the room. Now come back and sit down again. Close your eyes and picture the room. Tell me everything you can see and remember. Keep your eyes closed and tell me all about the room. Now open your eyes and look around again. Were you able to remember most of the things in the room?

Seeing with the Inner Eye

(Use this exercise after the children are familiar with the intense seeing exercise. Children may sit or lie down for this exercise.)

Now let's see if you can learn to see with your inner eye. You can make your own pictures or movies with your eyes closed. Close your eyes and relax your body like we have done many times before. (Continue with further guided relaxation if necessary.)

And now breathe very slowly and push your breath across the world. *Pause about one minute.*

You can see with your inner eye now. You can make pictures with your inner eye as I tell you a story. But first I want you to put a magic circle around you. Draw a magic circle of light all around you. Always put the magic circle around you before you look with your inner eye.

And now pretend that you are in your bedroom and you walk to your closet door. And inside your closet is a magic door. This secret, magic door slides open and you are standing at the top of a giant slide. It is bigger than any slide you have ever seen; it has many twists and curves. You have your magic circle on you so you can safely slide down. Slide down that giant slide now, down and around, speeding down that slide. And when you come to the bottom of the slide you are standing by a lake. Go down by the edge of the water. You are standing by the water skipping stones across the lake. Watch the circles they make as they splash.

Now you see a boat coming towards you. It comes right up to the edge of the lake and you climb on the boat and sail off. You are having a great time on this boat now, sailing along on the boat.

And now the boat comes to stop at the other side of the lake. And you climb out of the boat and walk across the field. This is a special field that you have made with your inner eye. You can come to this field anytime you want, just by closing your eyes, putting the magic circle around you and sliding down the giant slide. Now stay in this field and play for a while. You can play alone or bring friends here to play with you. Remember everything you do and tell me in the morning. (Or you may pause five minutes and then say, make the field disappear, and open your eyes.)

On my son Jake's first trip to the field he sailed across the lake on a huge sailboat that had a kitchen and a bedroom inside. It had both motors and sails. This wonderful boat took him to the field where he played tennis. He defeated Jimmy Connors and then sailed off again for England where he played Arthur Ashe at Wimbledon. The crowds cheered him on as he won that match too. Once again Jake set sail and returned to his field where he was a member of the Celtics basketball team. Yes, another victory, and then off to Fenway Park where he was a switch hitter in the World Series. There was no stopping him as he moved on to the Olympics where he won a gold medal in the decathalon. The fantasy didn't end until he experienced the glory of performing as a rock star. He performed both individually and with a group. Jake traveled in a chauffeured car to protect him from his adoring fans. The chauffeur let him off at the lake, where he climbed aboard the boat and then returned by elevator to his bedroom closet.

Children readily accept their inner eye since they are so closely involved in a fantasy world. These trips are fun and relaxing, and they encourage creative expression. It is a way of helping children learn they can be what they want to be. It gives them an opportunity to try on new ways of acting, thinking and feeling. Children do this spontaneously but by guiding them you are placing a greater importance on this type of activity. Seeing with the inner eye helps develop the necessary concentration needed for later exercises such as energy protection. Inner vision stimulates reliance on one's own body/mind rather than always looking to a source outside one's self.

Using the field, children can safely explore their scared, angry or hurt feelings. Going to the field with a brother or sister and working and playing together can be helpful in dealing with painful, jealous feelings. Here a child can finish a dream or meet that scary monster and befriend him. The field is the place to meet the friend inside you, a child's conception of the Oversoul. In the field the child can express many parts of her personality. She can be an artist, a clown, a mountain climber.

DREAMS

Children dream vividly as they struggle to grow and become independent. Their fears and anxieties are released through dreaming. They try out new and creative ways of expressing themselves and find new dimensions and potentials.

Children usually remember their dreams and need very little encouragement to share them. Try making a habit of sharing dreams early in the day, maybe at breakfast. Or have each family member choose another member to tell their dreams to. Each one should share a dream and hear a dream. Children can also make dream books. I typed the dreams as my kids told them and each child had his own dream folder.

Exploring Dreams Through Fantasy

1. Confronting a scary dream character helps change the dream into something positive. First talk about the dream with the child. Then suggest that she try to speak to the dream character and ask what it wants. It won't

be scary because she will be awake and you will be guiding her. Remind her that her inner eye is a camera and that she makes the pictures. She can stop or start the pictures any time she wishes.

Guide her to relax by pretending she is an old rag doll. Have her breathe deeply and push the air across the world. Put a magic circle around her, and then slide down the giant slide. Now that she is in the field she can meet the dream character. As you are guiding her, have the child tell you what she is experiencing. Then guide her to return and open her eyes.

2. Children sometimes have frightening dreams in which they are being chased. They wake up before they are caught. They can learn to finish the dream and get away from the thing chasing them by turning around and asking what it wants. Say something like, "Let's see if you can finish this dream and make it turn out just right. You can see the dream again with your inner eye, and when the thing starts to chase you, turn around and ask it what it wants. Remember you are making these pictures and they can't hurt you." Now guide the child as above.

3. Finishing pleasant dreams gives a sense of satisfaction and completeness. Some examples of finishing a dream are: fixing a broken object, winning a game, finding out what is around the corner or where the train is going.

Suggest that the child finish her dream by saying something like, "Last night you had a dream you wanted to finish but you had to get up for school. Let's see if you can finish that dream now." Then guide the child to re-enter the dream as above. Guiding can be more specific if you wish. For instance you might say, "Now you are outside the house. What does the house look like? Now go inside the house and see what's inside? Who lives in the house?"

INTRODUCING THE OVERSOUL

Children, more readily than adults, accept the concept of guides or Oversouls. It is comforting to know that someone is always there for you. They like to feel older and important and meeting the friend inside helps them to do this. You can say something like, "Lots of times when you're upset, you really know what to do but you forget that you do. We all have a friend inside of us that helps us remember. We can visit her whenever we want. We can see the friend with our inner eye."

Don't worry that you are teaching your child to "escape" into a fantasy world and not deal with the "real world." It's important to learn to deal with life on many different levels. As long as your child has flesh and blood friends, seems relatively happy, eats and sleeps okay, does fairly well in school, you need not worry. The important thing is to provide a balance of inner (being) and outer (doing) activities.

Your Friend Inside

Deep relaxing, deep breathing, magic circle. And now you see your boat again and you know it is a very special boat, going to a very special place. This place is a secret island. There is no map to get to the island, but you know the way by heart. And on this island lives a very special person, your special friend. Your secret friend lives inside you and you can see your friend by going to this island. This special friend is just for you and knows you very, very well. Your friend is always there to help you and to play with you.

Your boat is sailing along now and you have almost reached the island. The boat has washed against the shore and you climb out on the island. Walk over to your friend's house and stay with your friend until you hear my voice calling you back. *Pause about five minutes.*

I'm calling you now, calling you back. Say good-bye to your friend, fly back to the room and open your eyes.

Magic Carpet, Secret Island, and *Magic Shoes* are three more fantasy adventures for kids.

Magic Carpet

Deep relaxing, deep breathing, magic circle. You are in the field now, running through the field. You run across the field and come to an old dirt road. Follow that dirt road now. Up ahead, along the side of the road, you see an old, old castle and as you come closer you see that the door is half open. And you walk into the castle and go to the stairway and climb the steps to the very top of the tower. You walk all the way up to the top of the tower and there are 237 steps to the top. *Pause one minute.*

And finally you reach the top and there is a little old woman sitting there in that tiny tower room. And she smiles at you and says, "I'm so glad you came to visit me." And she gives you a dusty old carpet. You are very polite so you take it and thank her. And then you unroll the carpet, and what a surprise! It is all woven with pictures and pretty, bright colors. You sit down on the carpet and the old woman tells you that this is a magic carpet and if you say the magic words, "Carpet, carpet, be my friend, carry me around the bend," the carpet will fly off, carrying you wherever you want to go. Say the magic words now and fly off on that carpet. Have a good time. *Pause about five minutes.*

And now fly back to the room you were in at the start of this story. Open your eyes and take a big stretch.

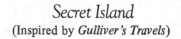

Secret Island
(Inspired by *Gulliver's Travels*)

Deep relaxing, deep breathing, magic circle. And now climb back onto your boat, your magical boat. You are sailing far across the ocean, far, far away to the secret islands. Enjoy your boat ride. *Pause about one minute.*

And now your boat lands on the first island. And you climb out to explore the island. And you see all the plants, trees and animals on the island. Finally you come to a village. But wait, look at this village. All the buildings are so tiny, so very tiny that you are like a giant in this village. The little villagers are running now. They are all coming to see you, the big giant who landed on their island. *Pause about three minutes.*

And now say good-bye to the villagers and walk back to your boat. You climb back into your boat and sail off, traveling to another island. And your boat reaches another island. This time you land quickly and run through the trees and who do you see but giants, lots of giants. Oh, but they are friendly. They are all happy to welcome you, a little midget to their island. One of the giants picks you up in his hand. And you are carried to the village. Have a good time visiting the giants. *Pause about three minutes.*

And now say good-bye to your giant friends and climb back into your boat. Sail back to the room you were in at the start of this story. And then open your eyes and take a big stretch.

The Magic Shoes

Deep relaxing, deep breathing, magic circle. And now jump up and down three times and you land beside an old dirt road. You poke along, wandering along this road, looking for nothing in particular. Suddenly you stumble over a huge box, half hidden in the tall grass. You open the box and inside is another box. You open that box too, and still there is another box. You open that box and look it's another box. Finally you open the last box and in it is a new pair of sneakers. They seem almost to jump into your hands. Quickly you take off your old shoes and put on the new ones. They fit perfectly. You run a little just to test them, then you jump. These sneakers are pretty good. Suddenly from around the bend comes a gang of bigger boys. One of the big kids comes over to you and says, "Hey, where'd ya get those shoes?" You start to back away and he follows; they all follow. You begin to run and the kids are right behind you and suddenly the next thing you know, you're off and flying. You've leaped so high that when you land, those kids are nowhere in sight. And off you go again for another adventure in your magic shoes. Have a good time. *Pause about five minutes.*

And now fly back to the room you were in at the start of this story. Open your eyes and give a big stretch.

HEALING

I started talking to my children about healing, telling them that their bodies are very strong. I said something like: "Your body knows how to take care of itself. When you cut your hand, your blood knows how to clot so the bleeding stops; then your body makes a scab to protect the cut and new skin grows. Your body is made up of energy, little tiny dots of energy always moving around. Some of the energy makes your blood, your bones, your muscles, your skin and everything else that is in your body. Some of the energy stays just as energy, those tiny invisible dots moving all around. When you are happy and eating and sleeping well then lots of energy moves around in your body. When you are unhappy or tired or eat foods that aren't good for you, then the energy gets stopped up. You can help yourself stay healthy by using your inner eye. With your inner eye you can picture the energy moving through your body. You can picture yourself strong and healthy and you will be strong and healthy." One of the first healing meditations I used with them was the shower of stars. To do this I asked them to pick their favorite color and that became the color of the stars.

Healing Stars

Lie down and close your eyes. Let your body become very loose. You are very relaxed. So relaxed you don't even move. And you are taking long deep breaths. Breathing the air in as if you were blowing up a balloon and then breathing the air out so the balloon is flat.

Your body is strong. Your body is so strong that it can take care of itself. Your mind is strong. Your mind is so strong that it keeps your body well. Good energy is all around you. Every time you breathe, you breathe in the good energy and it moves all through your body and it keeps your body well.

And now picture a big blue star over your head. A big blue star is over your head. Suddenly it bursts into thousands of tiny blue stars. A shower of stars pouring down on you. It is raining little blue sparkling stars. These tiny little stars are healing energy. When you take a deep breath, you bring the stars into your body. When you breathe out, all the little stars move through your body. All the tiny blue stars are moving through your body. You feel all warm and tingly as the stars move through your body. The blue stars are moving all through your body just like your blood does. They are moving into your toes and feet. They are moving up through your legs and hips. The blue stars are filling your stomach and your chest. You feel all warm and tingly as the tiny blue lights move along your back, all through your back, your shoulders, your neck. And now the tiny blue lights are moving into your head. The tiny blue lights will move all through your body all night and when you wake up you will feel strong and well.

During the time we began talking about healing and doing the healing exercises, we were also holding weekly family meetings. The purpose of the meetings was to make a safe place where we could all talk about feelings. Sometimes we picked a specific feeling, like jealousy. Many times these meetings were draining. Tears were shed and angry voices raised, but it got easier to be open about feelings and to recognize the good and bad things about each other, ourselves, our friends and school. The kids saw that it wasn't always easy to talk about feelings, but it was worth it. It was at these meetings that we also talked about why people get sick: how words can get caught in your throat if you are afraid to speak up and how this can result in a sore throat. They realized that sometimes getting a stomach-ache let them stay home when they didn't want to go to school. We decided that the kids had a right to take a break from school from time to time without getting themselves sick to do it. We instituted a bonus day program: every so often, they could stay home from school just to relax and play. This system has worked successfully for several years.

On the infrequent occasions when one of them felt sick we would form an energy circle and do a laying on of hands. The kids readily accepted both giving and receiving the energy and had no trouble in creating the images. Marc pictured tiny little men running into the body and turning hatches that let out air that would heal him. When Mike fell off his bike and cut himself, Marc pictured those same little men running into the cut with glue and gluing the skin back together. When Jake had a sore throat, Mike pictured little arrows running down his arm and out his hand and into Jake's throat. And when Marc had a fever, Mike pictured icicles cooling him so his temperature would go down. If the kids felt as though they were coming down with a sore throat or cold, they would go to sleep picturing the blue stars and saying, "When I wake up I will feel fine." I would go in and whisper the same thing in their ear, once they were asleep.

Another healing aid we used when they were younger was the pain stone, a small black stone that I'd found. When someone had a pain they would put the pain stone over the place that hurt and picture the pain going into the stone. When they were finished the stone would be washed, dried and put away for the next time. Sometimes it's easier to visualize if you have a concrete object. Try the stone yourself, it works!

ENERGY PROJECTION

Magic, to Jake, Marc and Mike, is learning how to use your mind and make the things happen that you want to happen. It's not pulling a rabbit out of a hat. That's a trick and they know the difference.

I began introducing energy projection to my kids by telling them that it was possible to make their minds grow stronger. Running, playing and eating good food will make their bodies grow stronger; learning how to concentrate will make their minds grow stronger. When you concentrate you think only of the thing that you are doing and nothing else.

When we all went bowling we would concentrate on getting a good score each time. Of course, we didn't get strikes all the time but we were increasing our ability to concentrate. We all concentrated for each other, too, and this helped cut down on some of the negative aspects of competition. We concentrated only to improve our scores; we didn't concentrate on making the other kids lose.

Concentrating saves time, also. If you can think only of your homework when you're *doing* your homework, it gets finished much sooner than if you sit there wishing you were someplace else.

Talking to their minds became a way of focusing positive energy. When Marc had trouble with math, he would take three deep breaths and then say, "Math is easy for me. I can understand this math." Then he would listen to the explanation and finish his homework. Don't forget to give your child time to gripe about how much work she has and how difficult it is. Then once the complaining is done (don't try to stop it; it's a good release) she can talk to her mind. When you tell your mind you know how to do something, your mind hears what you say and works harder to help you do it.

Affirmations are usually done at bedtime. If Jake has been studying for a science test and is worried that during the test his mind will go blank, he goes to bed affirming to himself, "I know all the answers on the science test." Then once he is asleep I go in and whisper the same thing in his ear. When the kids first moved to their present school, they were nervous about the change. I talked with them about it and then once they were asleep I would whisper, "School is easy for me. I like school. I have many new friends." The kids would always know beforehand what I would whisper, and often would ask me to come and whisper certain things to them. Our whispered affirmations have always been successful. When Mike was six, he was still wetting his bed. He went to sleep every night saying, "I will stay dry tonight." Once he was asleep I would whisper the same thing. After two weeks the wetting stopped.

RITUALS

We had done energy circles with the kids, and they'd had some idea of what happened during our rituals, but we had never shared a ritual together. Then one winter night, during a heavy snowstorm, the lights went out. The kids were very excited: this was the first time they had ever been without electricity. We lit the candles and then Marc said, "Let's do a ritual and make the lights come back on." We agreed, and Jake and Marc planned the ritual. Marc brought his shell necklace and Jake, his duck candle holder. A statue of the Goddess, some incense and a bowl of salt water were added. They wanted to share food and gathered some orange juice, wine, bread and rice cakes. The bread and rice cakes were broken into small pieces and placed in special cups. Jake brought some seashells and made a pentagram on the floor. Inside the shell pentagram were placed two candles, the necklace, the statue standing on a starfish, the salt water and the incense. Marc asked that we each hold a shell in our hands.

The candles and incense were lighted, and holding our shells we joined hands, so now we had a shell in each hand. We began humming, softly at first and then louder and louder. By squeezing our hands we would signal starting and stopping. Then we talked about the things on the altar. The duck, a swamp animal, had long been a symbol of the Goddess. And the shells, also Goddess symbols, have been worn as protection by many ancient peoples.

I suggested singing each person's name as we went around the circle. It felt self-conscious at first, but then it became very comforting to hear your name being sung over and over. Next we shared the food, passing the cups around the circle and soon we began feeding each other. The kids laughed at the thought that they and their parents were all brothers and sisters in the circle, but the excitement of creating something new yet so very old was obviously very appealing to them. By this time we no longer felt chilly, although the heat had gone off when the lights did. We joined hands again to concentrate on bringing the lights back. But somehow that no longer seemed important. The ritual had become an end in itself. Once again we hummed to join our energies. Then we opened the circle and went out to play in the snow.

When Marc was nine years old he entered his first boat race. He was somewhat apprehensive about it, although he didn't say so. We decided to do an energy circle every night for four nights before the race and concentrate on Marc's winning.

We cast a simple circle with seashells and placed in the center two green altar candles, one orange candle for Marc, a Goddess figurine, salt water, incense and a small red stone that Marc would carry for good luck.

The candles and incense lighted, I made the sign of the pentagram over each of our heads, explaining that it represented a person within a circle of protection. I pointed to the four corners and their corresponding elements on the altar (air, water, fire and earth), adding that the altar represents the deepest part of your mind.

Then we all joined hands and visualized Marc on the day of the race. I guided the visualization by suggesting we see the lake and the water, just a little rough. Then see Marc testing, and now the race is about to begin. The gun goes off and Marc is ahead the first lap. And now it's the second and he's still ahead, and the third lap and he won. See his face, look how happy he is, see everyone cheering.

The second night we cast the circle and proceeded as before. Then I spoke about how fear can sometimes make it difficult to concentrate. I suggested that we each write down what we were afraid of and then read the fears out loud. Next we would burn the paper saying, "As this paper is destroyed, so is my fear." Then everyone would add, "So be it."

I began reading, "I am afraid Marc will be nervous and upset and not have any fun." Marc spoke up, "That's right, I sure am nervous. That could really happen." Then Mike read, "I am afraid the boat will crash." Marc was listening intently and added comments as each person read. Anne read, "I am afraid Marc will be hurt." And then Marc, who had asked to read last, said "I am afraid I will crash and the boat will tip over."

Then we joined hands and visualized the race again. The next two nights we again created the circle and burned our fears. We realized that what we wanted was not for Marc to win, but for him to enjoy the race and be able to say that he was scared, for all of us to say that we were scared.

CHAPTER TEN

Witchcraft

Feminists, working to reclaim a positive image of female consciousness, are digging back to our roots. These excavations have led us into matriarchal time, a time when our foremothers had a very strong and valuable effect on each other, themselves and society. It was a time when women's values were the predominant values, a time when ancient women walked in harmony with their inner, cyclical natures, a time when women valued their intuitions and dreams.

One of humankind's oldest religions is Wicca, craft of the wise. Wise Ones—or witches, as they are more commonly known—worship the female creative force in the form of the Great Mother. The Great Mother, revered Creatress of Life, was the dominant figure for thousands of years. The worship of the Great Mother spanned the world and Her names were legion: Nut, Isis, Ishtar, Inanna, Diana, Hecate, Artemis, Selene, Demeter, Astarte, Hathor, Aphrodite, Kali, Bellona, Harmonia, Shin Moo, Rhea, Luna, Cybele, Trivia, Cerridwen.

The male force was secondary and was introduced much later as the son/ lover. He was her consort; she the immortal mother of a mortal son. The horned god appeared as a later personification of nature, but the female principle, the Moon Goddess, was the Queen of Heaven. In all ancient Babylonian and Sumerian creation myths women and men were created together in pairs by the Goddess. Female and male values were not polarized then. The male was part of the female, and female and male doubled in power by manifesting side by side.

The witches' concept of a god is the life force of the universe. Feminist witches worship this life force as a triune Goddess—Artemis, Selene and Hecate—the maiden, the mother and the crone. The three-formed Goddess has also been identified with the three phases of the moon: Artemis, the waxing; Selene, the full; and Hecate, the waning. Each phase represents another manifestation of the life energy, so that the generating, the organizing and the destructive aspects are all included.

The female principle is an agent of transformation: she is both creator and destroyer. Hatred of the female principle stems from a fear of death. When we come to realize that death is only a transformation, not an end, it will no longer hold any fear. Witches do not accept death as a finality, nor do they conceive of any heaven or hell in the Christian sense. They accept, as do many other ancient religions, the reincarnational process.

Witches believe in magic. Magic is knowing that the world consists of more than the physical reality. Magic does not work against nature: rather it is a deep understanding of the highest workings of nature and a movement in accordance with it. The object of magic is not to tell the future, to communicate with the spirits or to make one's will work for various ends. These are only the means. A witch develops her powers of magic in order to develop herself. Magic requires that we begin to change the world by first changing ourselves.

Witches, acknowledging that the world is composed of more than physical reality, realize that humans also possess more than the five senses. The sixth sense, the psychic sense, which is latent in all of us enables us to connect with the world beyond the physical.

To learn the craft of the wise is to develop the powers of the deep mind. As these powers are developed, one has access to spiritual and psychic information and energy. Psychic sensitivity alone, however, will not develop the powers of the mind. Self-control and a strength of character must be combined with psychic awareness.

Witchcraft is more than a religion and the practice of magic. It is a philosophy, a way of life. Witchcraft offers us a beautiful synthesis of female and male energies. It integrates thought, feelings and intuition and provides a meaningful connection between the material and non-material worlds.

Witches celebrate each month when the moon is full, a time of great psychic energy. These celebrations are called "esbats." *Lady of Silver Magic* is a guided fantasy which enables you to create and experience a full moon ritual or esbat. Several elements of the ritual are included:

1. Casting the circle. Rituals are most often performed in a circle, symbol of the uterus, the creative force. Many elements of nature occur in a circle: the cycle of the seasons, the shape of the earth, sun and moon, the orbits of the planets. The circle is a place sacred and apart from the physical world. According to ancient Wiccan tradition, the circle is nine feet in diameter. When I cast circles, however, I am interested in creating a special space, not in the exact dimensions of the circle. The circle may be delineated by drawing it with chalk or by spacing stones or other objects, or by sprinkling water or salt, or by walking around the edge of the circle with incense, or any combination of these.

2. **Invocations to the corners of the universe.** Each compass point represents a different manifestation of energy or power. The North is the magnetic center of the universe. If you do any creative work it should be done facing north in the natural northern light. (For example, my writing desk faces north.) The Eastern corner is the symbol of all life, all beginnings. The South represents fire and passion, the life-giving energy of the sun. The Western corner symbolizes the waters of renewal. The sun seems to sink in the west and each day is born again out of the east.

3. **Inviting the Goddess.** You open yourself to the Goddess, the creative force of the universe.

4. **Opening the circle.** When the ritual is completed the Goddess and the powers of the corners are thanked and the circle is opened.

Lady of Silver Magic

Relax, deepen and protect yourself. Float down now to a deserted beach. Here on this quiet beach lighted by the moon you sit and watch the moonbeams sparkling and shimmering across the water. The sparkling beams dancing on the waters carry you even deeper. And you begin a slow and steady walk. Winding your way along the shoreline, your path guided by the moon. And you feel once again that irresistible pull that draws you to her, Lady of Silver Magic.

And that magical force, shows you that you are in her presence. Whisper to her, lovely Lady of Silver Magic. And in so doing, you, her faithful daughter, find joy, serenity and peace in her presence.

Feeling that force rising within you, your pace quickens and you are pulled along, pulled as the tides are pulled, drawn back to the time of the great matriarchies, an age that is past, present and future all in one.

And ahead of you is a small grove of trees. Entering that grove now you remember a time when you were one of the wise ones and that time is now. The trees seem to part and there in the clearing is the space where your sisters gather once in the month "when the moonswell fills to brimming."

Together you silently gather the stones and begin to mark off the circle and build the small altar in the north corner.

And drawing the circle from east to north, the women, each in turn, enter the circle.

The fire is lit and facing the altar you speak: "My Lady of Silver Magic, I do build this circle, a space sacred and apart, in your honor."

Taking a torch and lighting the east you say, "Beautiful Lady of the Winds, the skies are yours. May I become as free as you."

Taking the torch and lighting the south you say, "Oh Goddess of warmth and fire, the seasons are yours. May each spring bring forth the richness of the natural world."

Taking the torch and lighting the west you say, "Oh, Lovely One, the sparkling waters are yours. May the streams and rivers continue to flow clean and pure."

Taking the torch and lighting the north you say, "Oh, fertile lush Goddess of the earth, ancient mother who nourishes, who gives birth to all living things, the earth is yours. May it stay fertile and rich and free from spoil."

Facing the altar once again you speak, "Beautiful Ancient One, bless your daughters with your presence. Fill us with your light and love." All gathered now meditate on Her presence. *Pause about three minutes.*

Face the north and slowly extinguish the torch thanking the Goddess for Her presence.

Face the west and slowly extinguish the torch thanking the Goddess for Her presence.

Face the south and slowly extinguish the torch thanking the Goddess for Her presence.

Face the east and slowly extinguish the torch thanking the Goddess for her presence.

And facing the altar a final time you thank the Goddess for strengthening you with Her presence and slowly extinguish the fire.

Share farewells with your sisters and then quietly leave the grove, returning to the beach. And winding your way along the shoreline you move up and back to your usual waking reality. Return relaxed, refreshed and filled with energy. Take your time and then open your eyes and stretch your body.

Earth, Water, Fire and Air is another guided fantasy in which you travel to the Great Plains and evoke the winds, feel the wetness of the rain, the richness of the soil beneath your feet and the warmth of the sun. For some of us, many years of city living have dimmed our deep and abiding connections with nature. Although we can't always go to the plains, we can evoke that special feeling within ourselves and renew our connections with the universe. Ancient peoples lived in harmony with the earth, directly experiencing her cycles and seasons. They listened to the wind and it spoke to them; they were cleansed by the rains and healed by the energy of the sun.

The Plains Indians referred to the four compass points as the "Powers." Each power was represented by a color and an animal. The power of the north is wisdom, represented by the color white and the buffalo. The south is the power of innocence and trust, symbolized by the mouse and the color green. The east is the power of illumination, represented by the eagle and the color yellow. The power of the west is introspection, symbolized by the color black and the bear. Each of us comes into the world with one of these attributes or powers. We may be able to see things closely like the mouse or have the far-sighted vision of the eagle. We may have the wisdom of the buffalo but lack feeling and warmth. If we continue to see things only through one viewpoint we are not whole. We must learn to travel around the circle—or medicine wheel, as the Indians call it—and understand the world through many different viewpoints. There are seven powers in all: the fifth is the earth, the sky is the sixth and the seventh is the universal harmony. Of course, all of the powers of the universe are really one power: the peace and harmony that come from knowing yourself, your relationship to others and to the universe.

Wiccan tradition identifies each corner or power by several Goddesses, each possessing a different attribute. Each of the four elements is always represented in their rituals. Candles represent fire, incense symbolizes air, salt represents the earth and water represents itself. Salt water may be used, thus combining the water and earth elements.

Although most religious traditions personalize the creative force by giving it a female or male form, it is possible to sense this force without doing so. This energy is a part of us, not separate and outside of us. We each have our own ways of experiencing this energy: the importance lies in acknowledging the life force, not in the personification of it.

129

Earth, Water, Fire and Air

Relax, deepen and protect yourself. And now focus on my words and let them carry you back, back to a time and space where you are at one with the rhythms and cycles of nature, moving back to that space of understanding and intuitive wisdom. The womanwisdom of growth and change, nature's wisdom, the natural law, the wisdom of the tides and their ebb and flow, the spontaneity of the seasons, the harmony and the direction.

Find yourself now on the Great Plains, your feet digging into that fertile black soil, sinking deep into the richness of the earth. The earth, mother of us all. Lie down and embrace the earth, the ancient mother who nourishes, who gives birth to all living things.

And rise again and hold to you those connections, turn and evoke the east winds saying, "Hail to thee, powers of the east. Corner of all beginnings. Ea, Astarte, Aurora."* And the east wind rises to answer. And then again stillness.

Turn again and face the south evoking the winds saying, "Hail to thee, powers of the south. Corner of great fire and passion. Esmeralda, Heartha and Vesta." And the south wind rises to answer. And then again stillness.

Turn again and face the west evoking the winds saying, "Hail to thee, powers of the west. Corner of the waters. Aphrodite, Themis and Tiamat." And the west wind rises to answer. And then again stillness.

Turn again and face the north evoking the winds saying, "Hail to thee powers of the north. Corner of all powers. Demeter, Persephone and Ceres." And the north wind rises to answer. And then again silence.

And now far off on the horizon you see dark clouds forming. The sky is darkening. The clouds are moving swiftly. And suddenly the rain comes, at first gentle drops and then it grows heavier and heavier. The rain is streaming down upon you, and you cry out to the winds and the rain. And suddenly the rain stops. Your body is cleansed and purified.

---

*Invocations to corners adapted from Z. Budapest, *Feminist Book of Lights and Shadows* (Oradell, New Jersey: Luna Publications, 1976).

The sky is clear and the sun shines down upon you. Let in the healing light of the sun. Feel the warmth of its rays streaming down upon you.

And you remain in a calm meditative pose, having communed with nature, felt the warmth of the sun, the cleansing waters of the rain, the clean breath of the wind and the coolness of the earth beneath your feet. And you are thankful.

And you sense and feel this connection again and again and you seek to recreate them in your rituals. And in your rituals you represent the elements air, water, fire and earth. And these elements have been represented in rituals since the beginning of woman.

And now you leave the Great Plains and travel, up and back to your usual waking reality. When you return open your eyes and stretch your body.

The witches' calendar is divided into eight Sabbats or ritual celebrations. There are four Greater Sabbats and four Lesser Sabbats. These Sabbats are times of celebration and enjoyment; each ritual pays homage to a particular Goddess.

The four Greater Sabbats are: Candlemas, or the Feast of the Flame (February 2), the celebration of the waxing light, sacred to the Goddess Bridget, the time to initiate new witches; May Eve (April 30), celebration of the maiden Goddess Flora's coming of age; Lammas (August 1) celebration of the Goddess of Plenty, Habondia, and the Indian Corn Mothers, Kore and Ceres; and Hallowmas (October 31), celebration of the new year, sacred to Hecate, the Goddess in her third aspect as Destroyer of Life.

The four Lesser Sabbats are: Yule or Winter Solstice (around December 21), celebration of the birth of the Sun Goddess, Lucina; the Spring Equinox (around March 21), celebration of Persephone's return and her reunion with her mother, Demeter; Midsummer Night or Summer Solstice (around June 21), celebration of the Fire Queen of Love, Heartha, Vesta, Rhea and Artemis; Samhain or the Fall Equinox (around September 21), the witches' Thanksgiving.

The next exercise is a guided fantasy called *Winter Solstice.* This sabbat is also known as Yule, a derivation of the old Norse word "Iul," meaning wheel. The wheel is the Great Wheel of the Zodiac which turns as the seasons turn. Yule is the longest night of the year, and from that night on the nights grow shorter as the wheel of the seasons turns toward spring. We light our candles to symbolize the energy needed to turn the wheel, to lengthen the days. The rebirth of the sun, giving warmth and light is always cause for celebration.

I used this fantasy with my moon circle the night of the Winter Solstice. After casting the circle and invoking the corners, we all formed a wheel with our heads in the center. Then we moved into the trance state, traveled deeply within and discovered a gift. When we returned to our usual awareness we shared our gifts and continued our ritual celebration.

Winter Solstice

Relax, deepen and protect yourself. Tonight is the night of the winter solstice, the longest night of the year. And on this night you are alone, walking through the woods. Here the air is cool and crisp, there is a light snow falling, swirling down and around. You continue your wintery walk, your path lighted by the moon, her silver beams so bright it seems almost daylight. Yet the feeling is of night, and there is a stillness, a joyful expectancy in the air.

You continue along your wooded path and soon come to a clearing. Here, in the midst of the clearing, is a small cabin. Someone beckons you to enter, yet no one is there, no one that you can see. Still you can feel the presence very strongly. You light a fire to warm yourself and soon the light and warmth of the fire fills the small cabin. As you watch the flames dancing and the warm thick smoke rising into the air, you begin to feel drowsy, very drowsy, and soon you fall into a deep trance-like sleep.

There is blackness all around, so dark, so very dark. And it is becoming colder and colder. Yet the cold does not seem to affect you as you realize you are descending down into the earth, deep into the center of the earth. Here on this night, this long, dark night, you are moving through a tunnel, a long and narrow tunnel. It is so black that you cannot make out any shapes at all, you cannot discern where you are, you only know that you are sinking into a deep abyss, spiraling down and down.

Then out of the inky black space comes a tiny ray of light, very small, flickering faintly, almost dying, yet not quite. You begin to fan the light with your hands. You breathe into the light, your breath fanning the flames and they begin to grow, to glow brighter, and soon the space around you is filled with light, a sparkling, glimmering light. You see into the glow of that light a gift. A beautiful gift, a gift you have created. You have breathed it into existence. *Pause about two minutes.*

And now carrying and letting it be carried, you and your gift rise up, moving back through the tunnel, back into the cabin. And you know the longest night is over. And you have kept the light burning as did your mother Lucina of long ago. And you can return to the room now, bringing your gift to share. And you will return easily and gently. When you are ready, open your eyes and stretch your body.

The next three exercises utilize moon symbolism. Primitive peoples have always connected woman's nature with the moon's. Each has a monthly cycle of approximately the same length. The word for menstruation and the word for moon are very similar in many languages. (*Mens* means moon; in Germany the menstrual period is called "the moon" and in France *le moment de la lune*.) The moon, called the "Lord of Women," was the protector and guardian of all women's activities. Ancient peoples held that women alone, under the protection of the moon, could cause things to grow. So planting, cultivating and harvesting were all women's tasks. "The worship of the moon is the worship of the creative and fecund powers of nature and of the wisdom that lies inherent in instinct and in the at-oneness-with the natural law."*

The names of the Moon Goddesses are legion, yet their characteristics and attributes show us that they are one and the same. All Moon Goddesses are mothers of life. They are givers of fertility as well as destroyers of life. Each is a virgin, meaning one-in-herself. There is no male god who acts as her husband and rules her conduct. Each Goddess bears a son by what is called immaculate conception. When he comes of age they become lovers and consorts. Then the son dies and rises again. Often he is reborn as her son and the cycle continues.

The Moon Goddess has powers that are relative, not absolute. Under some circumstances they work for good and under others for evil. She sends the rains which bring forth vegetation and crops, but she also causes the floods and destruction. Like the moon, she lives her life in phases: the bright moon shows her to be beneficent and the dark moon shows her to be destructive.

---

*Esther Harding, *Women's Mysteries* (New York: Bantam Books, 1973), p. 35.

The Moon Goddesses were most often considered sources of higher knowledge and wisdom. This wisdom has been called the "Divine Sophia." The Greek word *sophos* means wisdom. Moon thoughts are fantasies, intuitions. They are not orderly, rational ideas. This kind of thinking comes not from our heads but from our innermost depths. Sophia is the highest incarnation of this female principle, this source of divine knowledge.

Mythology tells us that the inspiration of the moon comes from the dark moon and the soma drink brewed from the moon tree. The ritual of the soma drink brings the worshipper in touch with the eternal, immovable reality of the self. Drinking soma brings eternal life, inspiration and the wisdom inherent in nature. Nature's wisdom is the wisdom that knows without knowing how. It is not learned but instinctive.

Ashera, or the sacred moon tree, appears repeatedly in ancient religious art. It may be represented as a wooden pillar or an actual tree or plant, sometimes with a crescent moon in its branches. The cutting down of the ritual tree was often the reenactment of the death of a god. The moon tree is often decorated with fruits or lights, as is the Christian Christmas tree. Assyrians decorated the tree with ribbons, much as in later times others decorated maypoles. An ancient hymn of Eridu commemorates the sacred tree as the "house of the mighty mother who passes across the sky."

Moon, Moon

Relax, deepen and protect yourself. Moving down now, down and down, deep into the core of your being, the essence of your female nature. And you find yourself on a deserted beach under the light of the moon. Watching the moonlight shimmering on the water, feeling those moonbeams pulling you, drawing you back and back, back into your womanheritage.

Gaze at the moon and feel her force and power pull on your being. Know that primitive peoples believed the moon to be the giver of fertility. Mother of all living, shine on us now. Giver of life, all movement, all growth. *Pause about two minutes.*

Know the power of the moon, source of divine wisdom, giver of fantasies, dreams and visions. Bringer of creativity, originality, divinity, shine on us now. *Pause about two minutes.*

Know the power of the moon. Our power like hers is light and dark. Spirit of the underworld, shepherd of the stars, bringer of sleep, darkness and death. *Pause about two minutes.*

Know the power of the moon. Feel it wax and wane within you. Moon Goddess, She Who Shines for All. Ishtar, Mother of All, Opener of the Womb, Silver Shining, Seed Producing and Pregnant. Queen of the Underworld, Hecate, snake scales in her hair, Darkness and Sorrow.

Full moon rising within you as you listen to the words of the Great Mother. She says: "Whenever ye have need of anything, once in the month and better it be when the moon is full, then shall ye assemble in some secret place . . . to these I will teach things that are yet unknown. And ye shall be free from all slavery . . . keep pure your highest ideal; strive ever toward it. Let naught stop you nor turn you aside . . . Mine is the cup of the wine of life and the cauldron of Cerridwen . . . I am the Mother of All Living, and my love is poured out upon the earth. I am the beauty of the green earth, and the white moon among the stars, and the mystery of the waters, and the desire in the heart of woman. Before my face, let thine innermost self be enfolded in the raptures of the infinite. Know the mystery, that if that which thou seekest thou findest not within thee, thou wilt never find it without thee. For behold, I have been with thee from the beginning and I await you now." *

Waxing and waning, waxing and waning, gently moving up and back to your waking reality.

Moon Grotto

Relax, deepen and protect yourself. Move deeply within, move through long winding passageways, labyrinths, winding down and around until you come again to dark water lapping and there a small boat is tied. Climb into that boat now and float off through passageways and caverns, going deeper and deeper, conscious only

---

*Ancient Wiccan Invocation

of the rocking motion of the boat and the soothing sound of the water lapping, floating along through dark caverns until you come to a large grotto, your boat comes to rest at the circular edge of the lagoon.

Looking overhead you realize that this space is lighted by the moon, moonlight pouring down, reaching down into the grotto from a slender threadlike opening far, far overhead. And the shadows cast by that silver stream dancing magically along the walls of the grotto. And you know that this is a sacred space.

Here in this sacred and magical space you will meet Sophia, Queen of Heaven, Giver of Wisdom. She appears here once in the month when the moon is full, to share her knowledge with women who find their way into this secret space. She is appearing here now and you will spend some very important time with her. *Pause about five or ten minutes.*

And now leaving the grotto and winding back through the long dark passageways and then floating up and back to your usual waking reality. Remember all you have experienced and carry that knowledge with you. Return relaxed and refreshed.

Ashera, the Sacred Moon Tree

Relax, deepen and protect yourself. Deepening, ever deepening, until you reach dark water lapping, where a small crescent boat is tied. And now perceiving through the dim light symbols carved on that boat, you realize this is a sacred boat, unlike any you have ever seen. And you climb into that crescent shaped boat and sail off across the water, safely protected by the moon boat's magical symbols. And you sail on and on, through the misty night, watching the moonbeams shining on the water. Dimly at first and soon the beams become brighter, dancing brighter and lighter. Shimmering and dancing across the water and you know that your boat is guided by those silver beams. *Pause about two minutes.*

And now your boat gently washes ashore and you climb out and walk across unknown yet always known land. And you know you are journeying toward something of great importance. The journey is long and slow. You are becoming tired and thirsty but you keep moving onward, secure in the knowledge that something of great wonder awaits you. *Pause about one minute.*

And now in the distance you are able to distinguish the outline of a tree, a strange and magical tree. Coming closer you see that her branches are loaded with a wonderful looking fruit. Eagerly you begin climbing the tree until you come to rest in the curve of her branches. Hungrily you pluck a piece of this strange, new fruit. This is the fruit of the Goddess. The juice of this fruit brings inspiration and wisdom, the wisdom that knows without knowing how it knows. To drink of this heavenly fruit brings immortality. And as the honey-like juice of the fruit reaches your lips and you begin to swallow it you feel a hazy mist descending over you. Gradually you sink into a deep and dream-like sleep. And during this sleep you will have a vision in which the ancient mysteries of life will be revealed to you. *Pause five or ten minutes.*

And now remember that vision and carry it back with you as my voice beckons you to return. You will return filled with wisdom and inspiration.

Many feminist witches follow the Dianic tradition in which Diana is revered as the Creatress of Life. Diana means Holy Mother (dia=holy, ana= mother). The following exercise is adapted from Charles Leland's *Aradia, Gospel of the Witches.*

Diana

From the very beginnings of time all peoples prayed to the Creatress of Life, the Queen of Heaven. And she called herself Diana, Huntress of the Night. Diana was strong and whole, one-in-herself. She danced the dance of life and as she danced she separated herself into darkness and light. And the light became Lucifer, her brother. And seeing how beautiful this light, Lucifer, was, Diana wished to receive him again into her darkness.

Lucifer fled from her as the mouse flees before the cat. And Diana followed him into the night, followed him down, down to the earth. And watching him there, where he lived, and noticing his habits, she saw that each night as he slept, his favorite cat slept there also, at the foot of his bed.

And that night Diana, powerful as she was, was able to change bodies with the cat. Then when the night reached its darkest hour she assumed her own form and lay with her brother and thus became the mother of Aradia. In the morning Lucifer was angry but Diana charmed him with a spell, a song, a humming like the wheel of life. And so it came to be that all things are spun by the wheel of Diana.

Diana remained on earth but her magic was so strong she was unable to keep it from the people. She declared that she could darken the skies and turn the stars into mice. The people said if she could do this she would be their queen.

So Diana dug into the earth, scooping up handfuls of dirt and mice and put them into the bladder of an ox. Then she blew into the bladder until it broke. The earth that was in the bladder became the heavens and for three days it rained. The mice had become the rain and the stars. And Diana became Queen of the Witches, the cat who ruled the star mice.

CREATION MYTHS

How did the world begin? All religious traditions have sought to answer that question through creation myths. The earliest creation myths designate only the female as the creative force. In the beginning was woman. All life sprang from her womb. Helen Diner states: "Mythology has always known this: above the gate of the Egyptian Goddess Nieth it says: 'I am what is, what will be and what has been. No one uncovered me. The fruit to which I gave birth was the sun.' " *

Thalat was the original being in Babylonian creation myths who gave birth to a divine couple, Thiamat and Apsu, thus creating a second generation. In the earliest Greek myths, Gaea, the female earth, emerged from the primal vagina, "the abyss sensing everything." Gaea, the virgin Goddess, created Uranos, the sky, and together they founded the race of the Titans. The Vedic nature goddess Vac is the creative word from which all things emerge. "Vac means language. She is the maternal mouth cavity which forms and awakens the living word without being touched by a tongue as paternal phallus." *

---

*Helen Diner, *Mothers and Amazons* (New York: Anchor Books, 1973), p. 2.
**Ibid., p. 6.

A number of women are the main figures in the creative process in an Iroquois Indian creation myth. The myth begins with a woman becoming pregnant in heaven. A second woman becomes pregnant and falls to earth, landing in the water. She rises out of the water and gives birth to a girl. Only in the third generation does she give birth to a male, when she has twins. So here, too, the male appears much later, just as, in the Babylonian myth, Thalat in the second generation gave birth to Thiamat the female and Apsu the male who were torn apart to make heaven and earth.

There are countless creation myths that have a pregnant female who contains the whole world. Where there are no human figures, creation often comes from an undifferentiated mass in the shape of an egg, the female symbol (Brahma, the father of all worlds, lay hidden in an egg for a year and after emerging divided it into heaven and earth), or springs out of the depths of the abyss, clearly a primal vagina image.

The original great mothers were all Moon Goddesses. The Moon Goddess is the Magna Mater, and from her comes all fertility, prosperity, joy and love. Male gods began as children, dependent on the Great Mother. Half the gods of Asia Minor began as the mortal children of immortal mothers. The female is the first and primary principle of nature. The male is secondary and mortal.

All Mother Goddesses spin and weave, like Nemesis who sits in the center of the cosmos while the axis of the cosmos spins around in her womb like a spindle. The Goddesses weave the world tapestry and they weave the veins and fibers into human bodies. "Harmonia weaves the starry sky and Arachne pins all the romantic entanglements of gods and men in her net." *

Women of old could find in these great Goddesses a reflection of themselves, since Goddesses personify all the major attributes of womanhood. The Goddess is a validation of the psychic wholeness of woman. She is an archetype of nature and life and embodies the intangibles of feeling and instinct. She is creator, nurturer, healer, protector and defender, and she is the connection with the source of life and knowing.

Women have always been a civilizing influence, passing on remnants of the culture when the culture itself passed. The foundations of every society are based on the feminine principle of relatedness. Woman values the ties of blood and kinship. Woman loves her children as children of her body and children of mother earth. All are equal. Human life is sacred and dignified. There is great respect for the inner world of emotions and instincts. These are the principles of matriarchy.

Creation myths are often described as the deepest and most important of all myths because they deal with the most basic problems of human life

*Ibid., p. 16.

139

and are concerned with the ultimate meaning not only of human existence but the existence of the whole cosmos. When there is about to be a shift in conscious awareness, a creation myth will emerge from the unconscious. Of course, every new element of conscious awareness that first arises is met with conscious resistance, but if we become open-minded enough to let the new idea in, changes begin to happen.

In times of chaos, such as ours, the retelling of creation myths signifies the world being born again. To signify our rebirth we must retell the most ancient of all myths, the myths of the Great Mother Goddess. We are at the dawning of a new age of feminist awareness, and we must allow our own creation myths to emerge also.

I am including three modern creation myths and poems: "For D.M.," a poem by Karen Lindsey which came out of our working together; a selection from *Letters of a Midwife* by Sue Silvermarie, which portrays the birth of the psychic child, the self; and "Colors," a creation myth by Seija Ling. Hearing these beautiful myths and poems while in the trance state is a moving experience.

For D.M. *

by Karen Lindsey

alive as death
the dark night wonders what its name was
when there was only night, and the sun a silver dream,
an embryo of light unvisioned
in the black infinity.
when does the rich and manic void
spew forth the first defiant self
suckling the sun's great breast,
weaned and suckling, weaned and suckling,
naming, containing, blasting free again,
hurling its laughter back to the ancient night?
lightning piercing the dark. vanishing. piercing.
birth invents the day invents the self
the sun shrivels and dies
a dream of light
an embryo

---

*copyright 1979 Karen Lindsey

140

Sue of the Mountains for Martha of the Woods *

by Sue Silvermarie

In a cabin at the treeline of a mountain
Two women came ripe
On the same starred night
And agreed to midwife one another.
When their contractions came in turns,
Their eyes grew knowing with small smiles.
One would soothe with old poems
While the other's stare
Clenched the swaying lantern.
The mat under them was soon salty with labor.
They invoked the wind and for a moment
She cooled their drenched foreheads.
Once a pain took them under both at once;
They swam in the same depths
Without seeing one another.
And each was glad the other wouldn't fear for her.

During a hushed lull
Before the final push,
Their eyes met and acknowledged
Everything.

The two ripe women gave birth,
And brought dawn.
But no children's cries filled the cabin.
And two who were midwife and mother
And daughter
Arose to greet their sisters at the door.

Colors **

by Seija Ling

Before the sea was blue
　　　　or the sky
Before there were any
　　　　colors at all

---

*Sue Silvermarie, *Letters of a Midwife* (Milwaukee, Wisconsin, 1975).
**Published under the title "Hands" in *Womanspirit,* Spring Equinox, 1976.

There were sisters
The sisters were as close
        as two could be
They could even see inside
        each other
But they knew there were things
        they must find
So they searched for them
        they separated
They looked almost everywhere
Under a tree   in a cloud
But they found nothing
At last they became tired
So they returned to each other
They were reunited
The younger looked deeply
        at her elder
        and saw truth
And at that her sister's hair
Became the deep rich black
        of truth
Then the elder
    looked deep
    and saw
            imagination
And that her sister's hair
    became the soft and vivid
    tones of brown and yellow
They touched each other's skin
        and it became the
        lightest hue of feeling
They saw into each other's eyes
        and they became the
        blue of tenderness
They touched each other
    on the mouth

142

And there was created
　　　the red of love.

After the sisters discovered color
There was still no fire
And we needed warmth
The goddess in her tenderness
Rubbed her hand upon her genitals
　　　　　a spark
　　　　　and there was fire

In the Before Time
we placed ourselves in tribes
we called ovulums—
we place ourselves not by
the color of our skins—
our height or the size
of our breasts or shoulders—
we chose our ovulum by the
way in which we communicated easiest.

I was born in eyes—
a lovely place—but when trying
to speak—I would watch my
lonely hands—like broken birds
and I knew I must leave
to find the place I could
　　　　speak clearest
　　and be understood best
I gave precious eyewater to
my borning tribe as my farewell
and began my journey—

There were many adventurers
and tales—I came upon
2 ovulums—first mouth
and then body
But I soon passed through
having enjoyed my stays
I finally came upon hands—
I knew I belonged by a touch
on the shoulder asking
　　　　who I was

And a touch of my hand
　　welcoming me
I love it here—I must say that
from being known as the silent one
　　　　or closed eyes
in my borning ovulum—
I am now known as quite
　　a talker
and I am even one of the
　　twelve dancers—
a position usually reserved
　　for the elders—

deceit is forbidden here—
lying with hands
a strict taboo
but of course
there is still fighting
words of anger or frustration
hands chopping the air
sometimes flaming
but gestures
are sharp clean and clear
and expel the hurt
quickly and thoroughly—

and when it is over
there are always
　　　　the 2 truce rituals
the grasping of hands
and the
　　　　honest touching
which always
　　recreates
　　the peace.

RITUALS

To become whole we need to find a center, a space where we can gather
and focus our inner energy so that we are not continually shaken by criticism, demands or stressful situations. Traditional religious beliefs have mistakenly identified this as perfection, when what is really necessary is whole-

144

ness. My personal search has led me into feminism, psychic development, meditation, reincarnation, Wiccan rituals, yoga and a study of matriarchal consciousness. Out of this search I have created my own rituals that strengthen and center me. I borrow from many traditions, but for the most part the rituals well up from an inner source. And later, to my surprise and excitement, I find how similar they are to ancient traditions.

A ritual is a stylized series of actions, whether physical or mental, that are used to change one's perceptions of reality. It is a symbolic event that attempts to concretize an inner event. A ritual often begins and is performed long before an awareness of the meaning develops. A transformation of personality is implied in every ritual and a ritual is implied in every magical process.

The art of ritual is the discovery of how to make the best use of energy flows. There is strength in ritual. There is power in clarifying our actions, making them precise and then using repetition of sounds and movements to build the energy. We bring our energy in tune with the universal energy, thus experiencing our connections with the whole of the universe.

A ritual may be as simple as the lighting of a candle, or it may involve elaborate preparations. Rituals may include the use of some or all of these things: stylized movements, repetitive words, chants or song, objects, costumes, tools, foods, beverages or drugs. Each action, whether it is a repeated series of words, a gathering of special objects, a way of dressing, or holding the body in dance or repose, is meditated on, chosen and executed carefully and thoughtfully. Rituals may happen spontaneously, or each detail may be planned in advance. Most rituals contain elements of both.

In ritual you create in the microcosm what you desire in the macrocosm. Before performing a ritual you need to have your purpose and the reasons behind it clearly in your mind. These questions might be helpful in assessing your purpose: What do I want? Why do I want it? What will happen if I achieve my purpose? What will happen if I don't? How will my success or failure affect other people? Do I want it so much that I become fearful or tense and block the energy needed to achieve it? Do I really believe I can achieve it? Do I think I deserve to achieve it? Do I have whatever is necessary (energy, self-confidence, tools, time, material resources) to achieve it?

Once your purposes are clear you can begin to plan the ritual. There are several steps involved in planning and performing rituals, and each is important in its own right. The first and second steps are planning and preparing materials for the ritual. And the third and fourth steps are the inner preparation (meditation and/or fasting and purification) and the ceremony itself.

There are varying situations in our lives that we might want to ritualize: holidays or celebrations of special feelings or happenings we wish to keep positive. We might also ritualize situations we wish release from: pain or fear, sorrow over the death of a friend, confusion over the breakup of a relationship. Rituals might also be used to change a negative situation into a positive one such as self-healing or changing from a jobless state to an employed one.

I have included several rituals from each category, all of which I have performed successfully. The first is a self-blessing, a ritual of affirmation that can be performed monthly or whenever you feel the need or desire.

Self-Blessing. Gather together a white candle, a small bowl or cup of water and a stick of incense. Pick a quiet time and space. Light the candle and incense and sit quietly, letting all tension slip away and all worried thought leave your body/mind.

Dip your fingers in the water and touch your eyes saying, "Bless my eyes that I may have clarity of vision."

Dip your fingers in the water and touch your mouth saying, "Bless my mouth that I may speak the truth."

Dip your fingers in the water and touch your ears saying, "Bless my ears that I may hear all that is spoken unto me."

Dip your fingers in the water and touch your heart saying, "Bless my heart that I may be filled with love."

Dip your fingers in the water and touch your womb saying, "Bless my womb that I may be in touch with my creative energies and the creative energy of the universe."

Dip your fingers in the water and touch your feet saying, "Bless my feet that I may find and walk on my own true path."

Quietly reflect on the words you have spoken and feel yourself filled with a peaceful, loving energy.

When you feel complete, put out the candle. Empty the bowl and wash it carefully.

Stone Ritual. The ritual of the stone symbolizes a release from pain and a renewal of loving energy. Women sit in a circle with a stone in the center. All relax and focus on the stone. Then in a calm and meditative way the stone is passed from woman to woman. As each woman receives the stone she holds it in her hands and imagines that she is pouring her pain into the stone. When each woman has filled the stone with her pain, the stone is washed in a bowl of water and dried with a towel. The stone is again passed around the circle. This time, as each woman receives the stone, she holds it and fills it with loving energy. When each woman has filled the stone with loving energy, it is placed in the center of the circle. All meditate on the stone, becoming like the stone, released from pain and filled with loving energy.

Wishing Ring Ritual. This ritual is best performed on the full moon when psychic energies are strongest. Wiccan tradition states that "boons" (gifts) are granted at this time.

Sit in a circle and join hands. Breathe together and feel the energy flowing around the circle. When all are in a calm, meditative state gently release hands. Take the ring (that has been chosen beforehand) and pass it around the circle to the right. Each woman holds the ring and meditates on it. The ring is passed around the circle three times. At the fourth passing of the ring those who feel ready will make their wish known to all. The wish is stated three times. Those who are so inclined respond by saying "so be it." Then all women send energy, visualizing the wish being granted. The ring is then passed on until all who want to wish have done so. Now the ring is placed in the center of the circle and the women again join hands. Feel the energy flowing around the circle. When you are ready, release hands.

Menstrual Ritual. Gather together candles (one red and one white for each woman and two red for the altar) salt water, incense, a ball of red yarn, small scissors and a cup or sponge of menstrual blood. A circle may be cast if so desired using the incense and salt water to mark its boundaries. Light the red candles on the altar.

All join hands in an energy circle. After a few minutes release hands. Each woman in turn lights her candles saying, "This red candle signifies my strength, I bleed and am not wounded. This white candle signifies my pure spirit, I am virgin, one-in-myself." Next the menstrual blood is passed, women may dip fingers into the blood and mark a spot on their foreheads saying, "This is the blood of my body, the blood of renewal, the blood of life." Then the yarn is passed around the circle, woven in and out so that we are all connected, we are all one. Women may now sing or chant, share feelings about their womanhood, or do whatever feels right. Then the ritual is drawn to a close as women sing, "Woman am I, spirit am I. I am the infinite within my soul. I have no beginning, I have no end. All this I know." * Each woman then cuts a piece of the yarn and ties it around her wrist signifying our blood ties with each other and with the earth. The circle is then opened.

---

*Women's Oral Tradition

Ritual to Release Fears or Negative Feelings. To perform this ritual you need candles, incense, pen and paper, a container or cauldron to burn the paper, salt water. This ritual may be performed alone or with others. A circle may be cast if so desired.

Light the candles and incense. Sit quietly and allow yourself to relax fully. Now reflect on those fears or habits that you would like to release. Write each fear, habit or negative feeling or experience on a separate piece of paper.

Take the pieces of paper, one at a time and read them aloud. Then burn each one saying "As this paper burns, my fear is destroyed." You may want to see the negative energy transformed into positive energy. As you burn each paper, you may say, "This fire is transforming my worry into careful attention." When you have finished burning all the papers, sit quietly and reflect on all you have said and done. Feel yourself to be released from fears and negative energy and filled with love and joy. You might want to use the salt water and perform a self-blessing. Then when you are ready, put out the candles and carefully dispose of the ashes.

Ritual for Protection of House. (May be used to protect anything.) We performed this ritual for friends whose house had been broken into several times. Since the performing of the ritual they have had no more trouble and believe those responsible moved out of the neighborhood.

The inner preparation for this ritual consisted of looking at the psychic reasons for the break-in. Often the purchase of a new house is a time of crisis as well as joy. It may bring up fears around deeper commitments to each other, greater responsibilities and so forth. Each woman asked herself what fears, doubts and repressed feelings could be responsible for this. What was her responsibility based on karmic ties? Space was given to express frustration and anger, wanting to get even with the people involved.

Materials needed: candles, incense, salt water, pen and paper, cauldron to burn papers.

We cast a circle and invoked the four corners. Energy was raised through an energy circle. Then we all wrote down our fears and angers concerning the break-in. Each in turn spoke these aloud and then burned them saying, "As this paper is destroyed, so is my anger and fear." Then we talked about the need for continual release. We wanted to express our anger, yet not allow it to bind us to the thieves. When we felt clear we joined hands and blessed the thieves, asking them to go in peace. Then we walked through the house carrying sticks of incense and circled each window and doorway, affirming that the house was protected from all harm. We returned to the circle and joined hands filling ourselves with loving energy. Then the circle was opened, the ritual complete.

Ritual to Stop Harrassment. This ritual was performed several years ago by a group of us who had ex-husbands and were being hassled by them about money and child visitation. (None of us were actively involved in custody fights then, although some of us had successfully fought them previously.) This ritual was successful: none of us had any trouble for at least two years after. The ritual may be performed again, whenever needed.

Inner preparation for this ritual consisted of examining our fears over losing the children, not having enough money to survive, acknowledging our anger and hatred of the men involved and the need to release it. We wanted to create a ritual of protection and affirmation of ourselves, not a hexing or cursing of the men.

We used red and yellow candles, incense, salt, water and oil.

We all joined hands in an energy circle. Then we took our candles and rubbed them with oil and blessed them by holding our hands over them and saying, "In the name of Isis of a thousand breasts, may our spell be blessed. In the name of Diana Huntress of the Night, may our spell be strong. In the name of Hecate Queen of Heaven and Queen of Hell, may our purpose be accomplished." * We lighted the candles and incense on the altar. Each of us then took the yellow candles which symbolized our fears and wrote the name of our ex-husband on it three times. Each woman in turn spoke of her anger and fear and how she wanted the situation to change. Then we took our red candles, symbolizing courage, and lighted them as each woman in turn affirmed her courage, strength and the ability to bring forth that which she desired. We closed the ritual with an energy circle. At the end of the evening we each took our candles home and burned them until they were burned down completely. We then carefully disposed of the remains.

Candle Rituals. Simple candle rituals can be used at anytime for many purposes. I frequently light candles for friends to wish them success or health, help them through a crisis, remember them on birthdays or special occasions. I choose the colors according to the need: sometimes they are the woman's astral colors; other times the color represents her wish (for example green for healing, red for courage and strength). I burn the candles till they burn out. The constant flame reminds me to send energy whenever I pass the candle.

---

*Z. Budapest, *Feminist Book of Lights and Shadows.*

CHAPTER ELEVEN

Spirituality

Because of its misuse in patriarchal culture, the word "spiritual" often evokes confusion, anger and fear. It conjures up either blissed-out escapism or the worship of a traditional male god. Patriarchal religious traditions, both Eastern and Western, have placed women in an inferior and subordinate position. When a culture perpetuates a creation myth that excludes the female creative force, it is a culture that categorically rejects women. The misogynist beliefs of our society have been the cornerstones of philosophies and institutions that have fed on fear and guilt, that have preached denial, repression and punishment.

It is this kind of thinking that takes our energy and channels it in ways that oppress us, alienating us from our true selves. Male belief systems have served to keep people apart, to deny physical, economic and cultural oppression. Men have directed energies needed to create supportive, life-affirming systems into forces of death and destruction. In the name of submission, sacrifice and service, women's creative energies have been channeled into nurturing others, with little or no thought of self.

Furthermore, "spiritual" has been seen as existing in opposition to material, practical and political. This stems from the patriarchal dualistic mode of thinking which forces all experience into rigid either/or categories. Right/ wrong. Black/white. Good/bad. Female/male. Our culture, our values, the ways in which we define ourselves have been limited by these rigid male definitions. Traits that should and could be powerful and beautiful have become twisted, ugly and oppressive.

The ability to be passive, when used appropriately, is the wisdom of waiting; it has, in its extreme form, become stagnation and death. Meek has been thought of as weak instead of gentle and pliable—flexible enough to bend and change. We have been forced to be receptive to other human beings, so much so that we are often no longer aware of, or able to fulfill, our own deepest needs. Denied the space to experience our emotions freely, we become hysterical or depressed. True acts of humility have been viewed as acts of self-deprecation rather than as choices rooted in a sense of self so strong that one is able to see beyond one's own viewpoint. Submission, the powerful ability to let go and open oneself to the unknown, has been reduced to cringing and bowing down to male demands. Sacrifice has been mistakenly thought of as a surrender *of* the self rather than a surrender *to* the self and its many dimensions.

Traditional cultural expectations have usually denied us the expression of wholeness, those ecstatic moments when we move beyond ourselves and sense a connection with the universal. The mystic or transcendent experience has been taken from us, and, having no vehicle for it, we become disconnected and often schizophrenic.

The spiritual is yet another dimension of the self, a dimension no less real than the physical. The difference between them is in the ways that spiritual awareness is revealed to us. We come into close touch with the spiritual aspect of ourselves through dreams, myths, visions, intuitions, hunches and feelings. It is time to reclaim this quality and re-establish our deep and loving connections with the universe.

We cannot continue to live within the limits of reality as defined by the patriarchy. All of us are taught at an early age what we are allowed to notice, which of our experiences are to be considered real and valid. A child who sees "pretty lights" around people's heads is said to have a "great imagination," but learns as she grows older not to mention those things. What is real is the talk you had with your aunt on the telephone, not the talk you had with the person who flies into your room at night. Soon "imaginary playmates" are repressed or forgotten. In a society that has overdeveloped the rational, the concrete, the material, we have no tradition for the truly mystical and religious experience. In a culture that is almost wholly outer-directed and goal-oriented, we have received guidance only in *doing* and no guidance in *being*.

Spirituality has been confused with denial and repression. I am not suggesting an annihilation of the ego, as some religious traditions teach. I am encouraging you to make your ego more flexible, thus expanding your awareness to include all levels of existence. I am not denying or degrading the material plane, only suggesting that it is one among many planes and that we can travel from the earth plane to other levels and then back again. Spirituality isn't an escape from the world, but an expansion of the world. The spiritual dimension enriches and sustains us—it does not limit or deny us. Spirituality is a celebration of love and life.

Spirituality refers to ways of transcending the personal self and connecting with the universal. The ability to transcend is part of our human nature. Our evolution, our progress depends on our ability to dream. Without our dreams we would not be able to step outside ourselves and transcend our limitations. Imagination is the key to creation. With our thoughts and dreams we can bring anything into existence. Our source of originality and creativity is the divine spark within us. It is this creative/goddess essence that we connect with when we embrace the spiritual dimension.

Because our society is so action and goal-oriented we are deprived spiritually, yet the ways in which we seek spiritual awareness are still dominated by aggressive modes of behavior. We expect intense flashes and visions; we demand instant enlightenment. We are drawn to secret goals and rituals and become absorbed in complex, obscure philosophies.

Awakening is a gradual process. We must be alert to the ways in which we have absorbed the power-based or violent dynamics of the culture. It is essential that we learn to integrate a spiritual awareness with a political awareness. On the spiritual level, where "all is one," the emphasis is on similarities, connections and process. The material or political plane speaks of goals, actions and products: it emphasizes our differences. If we continue to split the process from the product, we again fall into the male dualistic mode of thinking and acting.

Women who have the ability to formulate a political analysis, and work to that end, often believe that "the end justifies the means." A spiritual awareness necessitates an understanding that you must be accountable for the means as well as for the ends. You can have a new way of acting as a goal, but if the way you attempt to reach the goal is through the old way of acting then you are moving in a vicious cycle and perpetuating the same kind of behavior you are struggling to eradicate. Hence, while confrontation is at times a legitimate tactic for bringing about change, it is not appropriate in every circumstance. Used exclusively, confrontation leads to a false sense of superiority, the "more politically correct than thou" syndrome. Such negative behavior stems from the male mode of competition. It still assumes power over people: it is a violent way of acting, and violence breeds more violence.

To understand the dynamics of power-based relating, it is necessary to look at some of the belief systems that perpetuate it. The first is the myth of scarcity. People who live by this myth are afraid that there won't be enough resources for everyone, so they try to grab and hoard as much as they can. People try to hoard love and attention as well as physical resources. Of course, hoarding stops the flow and resources are temporarily diminished, so it appears the myth is true. Scarcity is created by our psyches and then manifests itself in our power structures. Power-based dynamics feed on this myth. Fear and greed *create* scarcity. The connection with the universal whole is temporarily lost, and the earth's resources become ravaged. Now we must deal not only with the fear of scarcity but the conditions that this fear has produced—inequitable distribution of material goods and pollution of the land, water and air.

The second myth, and one that is a cornerstone of the patriarchy, is the myth of the half-person. People who ascribe to this belief experience a sense of incompleteness, and falsely assume some other person will make them feel whole. This encourages them to channel their behavior into search-ing for and trying to keep that other person, and in the process they give up much of their own power. The "romantic" relationship of women to men is typical of this lack of wholeness.

Finally there is the myth of linear time. If you view time as an absolute (rather than as an organizing activity of the mind), you will believe that your past molds and limits you. But, in fact, the past, present and future are continually restructured and rearranged according to your beliefs.

Some feminists are oriented toward cultural or spiritual change, and are very much interested in the process of growth and change through self-dis-covery. This orientation is helpful, but not without risks. It is easy to be-come so preoccupied with the individual process that the harsh realities of

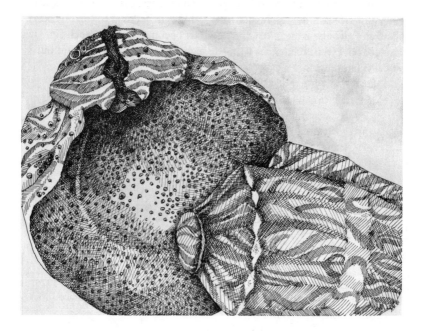

the patriarchy are ignored or denied. They become the feminist version of the the hippies of the sixties—"do your own thing" or "anything goes."

True spirituality, however, does not ignore the physical reality: it incorporates the physical. It is an awareness that embraces the self and its relationship to others and to the universe. As Dorothy Riddle has written: "We need the richness and strength of diversity, plus the focus and integrity which come from ideals and standards. We need both the freedom for process and the responsibility for product."*

The truths of a culture, the fundamental ways in which power is defined and transferred, are found within its religious beliefs. The Judeo-Christian myth has been rewritten to eliminate Lilith as the first woman. Eve, who was created second as Adam's helpmate, was named in her place. This myth exists as the justification for male domination and supremacy.** Earlier creation myths envisioned the creative force as female, giving birth to women and men simultaneously. During periods when the female deity reigned supreme, the role of women was markedly different from our present day patriarchal society.

The Judeo-Christian tradition, like most religions, has repressed the female creative force and denied us models for strong, independent and courageous women. We no longer have functional myths or living visions to show us what we can aspire to be.

Women's spirituality is both magical and mystical. It becomes magical every time we contact the higher forces, draw them down to the physical plane and give them creative expression. It becomes mystical each time we connect our physical energies with the higher energies and transcend our physical limitations.

---

*Dorothy Riddle, "Spirituality and Politics," *Womanspirit,* Summer Solstice, 1976.
**Merlin Stone's book *When God Was a Woman* (New York: Harcourt Brace Jovanovich, 1976) analyzes this myth in detail.

About the Author

Diane Mariechild, an Aries with Scorpio rising and an Aquarian moon, is a practicing psychic and feminist psychotherapist. She has degrees in education and counseling psychology (Goddard Cambridge) and has taught classes in psychic and spiritual development in the Boston area since 1973. Active in creating and celebrating womanrituals, Diane is the founder of the Dancing Wind Coven. She is the mother of two teen-aged sons.